HEINEMANN ADVANCED RELIGIOUS STUDIES

ETHICS & RELIGION

JOE JENKINS

Heinemann Educational Publishers
Halley Court, Jordan Hill, Oxford OX2 8EJ
a division of Reed Educational & Professional Publishing
Ltd

OXFORD MELBOURNE AUCKLAND
JOHANNESBURG BLANTYRE GABORONE
IBADAN PORTSMOUTH (NH) USA CHICAGO

Heinemann is a registered trademark of Reed Educational &
Professional Publishing Ltd

British Library Cataloguing in Publication Data
A catalogue record for this book is available from the
British Library

ISBN 0 435 30370 8

Cover designed by Red Giraffe
Typeset and illustrated by Tech-Set Ltd, Gateshead.
Printed and bound in Great Britain by The Bath Press, Bath

Acknowledgements
The author would like to thank the following for their
support and guidance: Robert Bircher, Jo Boyce, *Caduceus*,
Jennifer Johnson, *Jubilee 2000*, *Red Pepper*, Martin Rayman,
Mags Robertson, *The New Internationalist*, Jane Tyler and
Sue Walton and to David Jeffery, for his valued
contributions on pp. 18–19, 73 and 126–8.

The publishers would like to thank the following for
permission to reproduce copyright material.

Cassell plc for the extracts from *The Catechism of the Catholic
Church*, Geoffrey Chapman, an imprint of Cassell plc, 1994, on
pp. 60, 85, 91, 107; The Central Board of the Church of
England for the extract from *Responsibility in Arms Transfer
Policy (GS 1130)*, A Report by the Board for Social
Responsibility of the Church of England, copyright © The
Central Board of Finance of the Church of England 1994; The
Archbishops' Council 1999, and is reproduced by permission
on p. 123; HarperCollins Publishers Inc for the extracts from
Matthew Fox, *The Coming of the Cosmic Christ*, on pp. 29, 82,
103; London Examinations, A division of Edexcel Foundation,
for the exam questions on pp. 16, 17, 33, 41, 57, 77, 86, 95, 105,
117, 129; the Northern Examinations and Assessment Board
for the exam questions on pp. 16, 32-3, 41, 57, 95, 105, 117;
Oxford Cambridge and RSA Examinations Limited for the
exam questions on pp. 16, 32, 33, 41, 57, 77, 86, 95, 105, 117,
129; Resurgence magazine and Maneka Gandhi for the
extract on p. 76; SCM Press for the extract from *Situation
Ethics*, by Joseph Fletcher, SCM Press 1966, on p. 48; the
World Council of Churches for the statement on p. 69.
Scripture quotations are (except those acknowledged to
different sources in the text) from the Revised Standard
Version of the Bible, copyright 1946, 1952, 1971 by the
Division of Christian Education of the National Council of the
Churches of Christ. Used by permission.

The publishers would like to thank the following for
permission to use photographs.

Adam Shimali, p. 51; AKG Photo, p. 79; Andy Goldsworthy,
p. 1; Axel Scheffler, p. 61; Camera Press, p. 127; Charles
Dharapak/Associated Press, p. 43; Corbis, p. 49; David
Jeffery, p. 18, 126; Denis Farrell/Associated Press, p. 78;
Frank Baron/The Guardian, p. 71; Gary Calton/The
Observer, p. 89; Geoff Tompkinson/Science Photo Library,
p. 93; Hugh Warwick, p. 4; J.C. Francolon/Frank Spooner, p.
37; John McDougall/AFP, p. 122; John Schults Reuters/
Popperfoto, p. 104; Laguna Design/Science Photo Library,
p. 69; Lucia Chiraboga/Panos Pictures, p. 105; Mary Evans
Picture Library, pp. 19, 43; Nick Cobbing, p. 108; Nick Ut/
Associated Press, p. 118; Paul Bergen/Redferns Music
Library, p. 13; Peter Sanders, p. 16; Raghu Rai/Magnum, p.
113; Rex Features, p. 60; Robert Harding Picture Library, p.
75; Robert Todd, p. 27; Simon Townsley/Camera Press, p.
13; Teekee Tanwar/AFP, p. 100; The Guardian, p. 112; Wana
Gang Feng/Panos Pictures, p. 82.

The Publishers would like to thank Tony Stone Images for
permission to reproduce the cover photograph.

The publishers have made every effort to contact copyright
holders. However, if any material has been incorrectly
acknowledged, the publishers would be pleased to correct
this at the earliest opportunity.

Contents

The world of ethics

PHILOSOPHY

ETHICS is a branch of philosophy, 'the love of wisdom' which aims to understand the meaning of life and the nature of knowledge, beauty and goodness.

> *Philosophy is to be studied, not for the sake of any definite answers to its questions, since no definite answers can, as a rule, be known to be true, but rather for the sake of the questions themselves; because these questions enlarge our conception of what is possible, enrich our intellectual imagination and diminish the dogmatic assurance which closes the mind against speculation; but above all because, through the greatness of the universe which philosophy contemplates, the mind also is rendered great, and becomes capable of that union with the universe which constitutes its highest good.*
>
> Bertrand Russell, *The Problems of Philosophy* (1912)

Fig. 1.1   Philosophy is to be studied for the sake of the questions themselves

Faced with choices about sex, relationships, money and so on, we are constantly challenged to make '**moral** judgements' about others and about ourselves. It would be impossible to live a relatively ordered life if some of our principles did not match other people's ideas about right and wrong. Society would be a complete nightmare if it did not maintain some values upon which people were able to rely. Trying to make moral sense of our personal life makes modern living an intense experience. Thinking for ourselves is not easy, particularly as we are continually faced with the 'this is right, that is wrong' message from advertisers, politicians, peer pressure, religions, families or local street culture – and, as the Prussian philosopher Friedrich Nietzsche (1844–1900) reminds us in *Thus Spake Zarathustra*, '... at least every one claimeth to be an authority on "**good**" and "evil".' But are we really?

Sometimes we say or do things which we feel all right about at the time but on later reflection think wrong. Perhaps we feel something is wrong, but because of our desire to be attractive or to get a job or to impress our friends we may say or do something that fundamentally we believe to be wrong ... or think is wrong. We are constantly caught in a world of moral dilemmas.

Definitions

In ordinary language the words ethical and moral, unethical and **immoral**, are often used interchangeably. Popular thinking sees morality as simply about old-fashioned rules designed to stop people enjoying themselves, usually in relation to sex. This is a very narrow view, for ethics explores the values lying behind choices, the reasons given for these choices and the language used to describe them. It is about seeking the 'good life' – not being a 'goody goody' but *living a life that is real*, authentic, successful and excitingly responsible. It is about the dilemmas of life: relationships; sex; medicine; money; work; law; power; violence; the future. It is ultimately about *the art of living successfully* which the Ancients called 'wisdom'.

The range of issues that have implications for ethics is immense and varied. However, it is a mistake to think that ethics is a single coherent body of knowledge and opinion about what is right or wrong. In philosophy the term ethics is also used to refer to a specific area of study: the area of morality which explores human conduct and values. When we speak about people as *moral* or *ethical* we usually mean that they are 'good' people, and when we call them *immoral* we mean that they are 'bad' people. However, the simplicity of these definitions ends here.

How do we know what is right or wrong; how do we define good and bad? These sorts of questions make up the greater part of the study of ethics. Not everybody has a sense of what is right or wrong. The word **amoral** means having no moral sense, or being indifferent to right and wrong (this might include babies, or people who have been given prefrontal lobotomies). Some things are outside the realm of morality altogether (for example inanimate objects such as a stick are **non-moral**). A person using the stick, however, may use it immorally (by hitting somebody with it); but the stick itself remains nonmoral.

Ethical principles

The question 'What is Good?' has intrigued philosophers down the ages, and continues to do so today. Goodness in conduct has been viewed according to two chief principles: firstly, certain types of conduct which are *good* in themselves (implying a final value or **summum bonum**, which is *desirable in itself* and not merely as a means to an end), for example 'You shouldn't steal

whether you believe in God or not'; and secondly, types of conduct which are good *because they conform to a particular moral standard*, for example not stealing is good because it follows God's commandments. There have been three principal standards of conduct proposed by philosophers:

a happiness or pleasure
b duty – virtue or obligation
c perfection – the fullest harmonious development of human potential.

Authority

Depending on a society's social and cultural background, the authority invoked for good conduct comes from one of the following: *the will of a deity* (when obedience to the divine command-ments in sacred scripture is the accepted standard of conduct); or *the pattern of nature* (the accepted standard is conformity to the qualities attributed to human nature); or *the rule of reason* (the best behaviour results from rational thought).

Autonomy

Autonomy refers to a person's capacity to choose freely and direct their own life. Autonomy is hardly ever pure but restricted by factors such as the law, social tradition, the autonomy of other people, and the prevailing circumstances of a person's life (for example age, background, personality). Personal autonomy depends upon a degree of knowledge sufficient to permit us to pursue an end; an understanding of the routes open towards that end, and of the pitfalls and the ways in which knowledge can be employed in order to achieve that end; and the possession of rationality to select appropriate ends.

Relativism versus absolutism

(see pages 96–8)

Relativism recognizes that a wide variety of ethical beliefs and practices exists. Today, for example, very different sets of moral beliefs are held by feminists and religious fundamentalists about sexuality and abortion. Differences in moral belief also exist between different countries and tribes and between different subcultures within a society. History illustrates how time alters moral beliefs. How can we prove that one belief is right and others wrong? Moral relativists argue that there is no way of deciding and there is no 'moral knowledge'.

Absolutism, on the other hand, holds that there does actually exist a set of universal moral rules that are always true. However, this has its dangers in that it can legitimize one powerful culture as it imposes its own local moral values on all others by claiming a monopoly on the 'moral truth'. European settlers in North and South America imposed their own moral truth on the tribal cultures (see pages 102–3), often justifying wholesale slaughter, slavery and the environmental destruction of lands held to be sacred, by maintaining that they had '**absolute** moral knowledge' about how these people *ought* to live.

Today most people would not want to interfere with other moral belief systems. They may even argue that although customs and practices vary, the underlying beliefs are the same. The sacrificial religion of the Aztecs in Central America, for instance, may be seen as reflecting a belief that ritualistic death is for the ultimate long-term heavenly good of the victims involved. The sanctioning of the murder of innocents for any other reason is not morally acceptable. Absolutists claim that beneath the forms of practice lies the essence of moral knowledge.

LINGUISTIC PHILOSOPHY – THE NATURE OF ETHICAL LANGUAGE

MUCH of the debate about ethics in modern philosophy has been concerned with the meaning of moral statements and the possibility of showing that they are either basically true or false. There are three different kinds of language used in ethics:

a Descriptive ethics *describe* the way we live and the moral choices we make. Descriptivists simply present facts, for example: 'Seventy-two square miles of desert appear on Earth every day'. The actual information may be correct or incorrect. It can be checked by referring to statistical information, environmental reports and satellite pictures. However, the statement does not make any moral claim about desertification, nor does it say whether it is a good or bad thing. A statement such as 'More money is spent on armaments in one day than the world's two billion poorest people have to live on in one year' again simply states a fact. It does not condemn or condone, nor even comment on this state of affairs. Some philosophers, however, argue that descriptive ethics can sometimes *imply* moral judgements by the way in which information is presented.

b Prescriptive ethics are concerned with prescriptions and norms about what is right and how people *should* live. **Prescriptivists** explore questions such as 'Should we act in our own self-interest?'. They might go even further and come up with definite, though not always identical, conclusions. For example, when looking at issues around the environment they may come up with certain prescriptions: 'Given the evidence, a person should always join movements that work against environmental destruction and the arms trade'; or 'People ought to act in the interests of the environment or boycott unethical businesses'; or 'People should always act in the interests of all concerned, themselves included'; or 'Desertification, leading as it does to famine and caused as it is by the policies of the rich world, must be stopped by the adoption of new policies by the rich world'.

These conclusions are no longer *descriptions* but have become *prescriptions*, i.e. they *prescribe* how people should behave, not merely *describe* how they do behave. Prescriptive ethics was considered an important part of ethics up until the 1930s when it became relatively neglected except for occasional discussions about **utilitarianism**. However, today, concerns about the environment, genetic engineering and worldwide economic injustice has meant that an increasing number of modern philosophers are looking for universal prescriptions to contemporary moral issues.

c **Meta-ethics** (analytical ethics) *analyses* ethical language. It looks at the meaning of moral judgements and analyses the reasoning behind ethical systems. It is concerned with the meaning of moral discourse and does not prescribe anything nor provide descriptions, concentrating on reasoning and language rather than on content. Instead of looking at practical issues, meta-ethicists limit themselves to studying the nature of morality and the meaning of moral judgements. During the twentieth century, meta-ethics became a major preoccupation of many philosophers, in part a result of the difficulties of formulating a system of ethics in a pluralistic world.

This obsession with language and logic, and the comparative neglect of contemporary moral issues, has sometimes opened up meta-ethicists to attack. Critics argue that in a fast-changing and increasingly dangerous world philosophers should be working out how they can help to create **universal justice** and peace, rather than wasting precious time arguing about definitions.

However, this is a little unfair. Any complete study of ethics needs to incorporate the descriptive, the **normative** and meta-ethical approaches. Ethicists need to draw on the evidence provided by psychologists, social scientists and environmentalists, etc.; they need to examine how language is used in ethical discussions; and they need to help us create systems that protect and nurture the old and the young, the poor and the dispossessed, enabling all faiths and all

peoples to live together in a tolerant and harmonious society.

Problems with the three types of ethical language

- Descriptive ethics – sometimes facts can be mistaken for values. You need to ask yourself what is the difference between a *fact* and a *value*?
- Prescriptive ethics – by arguing passionately that things 'ought' to be different it is easy to fall into the trap of preaching. This can be dangerous if it prevents somebody making a detached, reasoned and informed choice for themselves (**autonomy**).
- Meta-ethics – the chief danger with this approach is that it can become too much of an intellectual exercise, with philosophers losing sight of the real world, an issue explored in the 'is/ought' controversy.

Things to do

Write two captions for this photograph, one descriptive and one prescriptive.

The 'is/ought' controversy

This centres around the distinction between epistemology (theory or theories of knowledge) and prescriptive ethics. Epistemology is concerned with what *is* the case, whereas prescriptive ethics is concerned with what *ought* to be the case. Epistemology aims to describe, scientifically or logically, the way the world *is* constructed; prescriptive ethics aims to give an account of the way the world *ought* to be and the ways people ought to behave.

Many philosophers, from David Hume (1711–76) onwards, have maintained that there is a sharp distinction between epistemology and ethics, and to move from one to the other is problematic. There is a 'gap' between factual statements ('is' ones) and moral statements ('ought' ones), and to jump from a something 'is' statement to a something 'ought to be' statement is rather like jumping to conclusions. Some modern ethicists such as Pete Singer and Alasdair MacIntyre, however, argue that there *are* situations where it is logically acceptable to move from a descriptive statement ('is') to a prescriptive one ('ought'), for example:

- 'Is' statement: He *is* a vegetarian. (descriptive)
- 'Ought' statement: Therefore, he *ought* to do what vegetarians do. (prescriptive)

'Who I am dictates what I ought to do.' The bridging of the gap from descriptive ethics to prescriptive ethics has become more acceptable in modern philosophy, particularly around environmental issues (see pages 74–6). Also, philosophers increasingly concerned by the profound ethical implications of contemporary moral issues like genetic engineering (see pages 63–7) are putting less energy into metaethics and more into prescriptive ethics.

G. E. Moore's definition of good

> It appears to me that in Ethics, as in all other philosophical studies, the difficulties and disagreements, of which its history are full, are mainly due to a very simple cause: namely, to the attempt to answer questions, without firstly discovering precisely what question it is which you desire to answer.
>
> G. E. Moore, *Principia Ethica*

Philosophers, since Aristotle, have wrestled with the question 'What is the Good Life?' The British philosopher G. E. Moore (1873–1958), in *Principia Ethica* (1903) and *Ethics* (1912), asks the same question. Some theories of ethics had defined goodness in terms of some nonmoral position, for example in terms of pleasure, the good of society or fulfilling God's commands. This is a **Naturalistic theory of ethics**, and those who believe in this definition of goodness are called ethical naturalists. This theory however could apply to a situation in which 'good' is defined as 'what the Mafia wants'. In this case, protection rackets, murder and smuggling weapons could be called 'good' provided the Mafia wants them.

Moore maintained that 'goodness' is indefinable and no moral statement can be defined in terms of a nonmoral statement. He argued that those who defined goodness in this way committed 'the naturalistic fallacy'. Moore argued that ethics can only define one moral concept in terms of another moral concept. The word 'right', for example, might be defined in terms of the notion of 'good' – 'A right action is one that leads to a good consequence'. However, if ethicists try to define 'good' their only hope of doing so would be by bringing in the term 'right' or another term. The definition would then be circular and not a definition at all. Moore wrote that good is 'incapable of definition' because it is the 'ultimate term of reference by which whatever is capable of definition must be defined'.

Moore admits that good actions are, as a matter of fact, productive of pleasure. Some may even say that productiveness of pleasure is part of the meaning of the term good, but not the whole of its meaning, so that it cannot serve as its definition. Others may hold that what causes an action to be good is the fact that it produces pleasure, but a statement of what causes an action to be good is not a definition of goodness. Good includes something more than just productivity of pleasure, so 'All good actions produce pleasure' is a **tautological**

statement in which the predicate (pleasure) adds nothing to our understanding of the subject (good).

Moore believed that this argument can be levelled at any naturalistic definition of good, so when people say that good is commanded by God, they are not really defining good, because a good action could still be a good action even if it were not commanded by God. Goodness, maintained Moore, is just as indefinable as the word yellow. Both words, goodness and yellow, can be explained in terms of the results produced (for example yellow produces pleasure; good produces pleasure), but this is not the same as saying that pleasure is what good is, anymore than it defines the colour yellow.

Although Moore is asserting that good is indefinable, he has given no reason, and as such his claim is only an *assertion* and not an *argument*. Moore argued that because goodness is not like any other quality it cannot be defined. He thought that as soon as one tried to define it, the definition begins to reduce and limit the idea. This problem arose, too, when trying to define a colour – it cannot be done.

Logical Positivism

Ethical questions are at the very heart of life. However, according to one particular view of philosophy, **Logical Positivism**, such questions cannot be answered by moral philosophy. Logical Positivism (sometimes called Logical Empiricism) emerged during the early part of the twentieth century. Initially known as the Vienna Circle, the movement included R. Carnap (1891–1970), M. Schlick (1882–1936) and O. Neurath (1882–1945), whose works influenced British philosophers like A. J. 'Freddie' Ayer (1910–89), Bertrand Russell (1872–1970) and Gilbert Ryle (1900–76).

Ryle summed up the view of those influenced by this type of philosophy when he said in 1932: 'The main business of philosophy is the detection of the sources in linguistic idiom of recurrent misconceptions and absurd theories.' The Vienna Circle three years previously had outlined their task: to establish criteria so that philosophers could *talk meaningfully* about the world. According to Logical Positivists, philosophy is about establishing how the truth or falsehood of certain propositions can be demonstrated. If a proposition cannot be established as true or false, then it is meaningless. By examining language the Logical Positivists concluded that there are three types of statements:

a Analytical or logical statements (for example 'All bachelors are unmarried men'). Ludwig Wittgenstein (1889–1951) called these types of statements tautological in the sense that bachelors is simply another way of saying unmarried men. Most propositions of mathematics or logic are analytical.

b Synthetic statements (for example 'John is a married man') are those that can only be verified or falsified by observation and examination.

c Meaningless statements (for example 'Violence is wrong'). When Logical Positivists call a statement meaningless they do not mean that the statement is sheer nonsense, but rather that it cannot be verified. For a Positivist, philosophy is essentially about theories of knowledge (epistemology). Ethics, aesthetics and theology do not constitute proper knowledge. They cannot be proved or disproved (unlike synthetic statements), because they are basically emotive (dealing with issues that are rooted in feelings of approval or disapproval, like and dislike, preference and non-preference). One of the most famous proponents of this view, the British philosopher A. J. Ayer, was sceptical about the possibility of ethical knowledge, and in his important book *Language, Truth and Logic* (1934) claimed that moral language is meaningless: '. . . sentences which simply express moral judgements do not say anything. They are pure expressions of feeling and as such do not come under the category of truth and falsehood.' For Logical Positivists, then, ethical or theological statements are meaningless because they are not empirically verifiable, nor are they obviously analytical statements.

In defence of ethical language

Such views shocked the philosophical world. If the Logical Positivists were right, then the study of ethics becomes a waste of time and energy. However, in the real world ethical language has significant meaning. We not only *feel* that the murder of children is wrong, whether it be directly by an individual or indirectly by government action, we also *know* that we are reasonably justified in saying 'The murder of children is wrong' and would be prepared to support our argument. It is plainly ridiculous to reduce morality simply to how we feel about something and ignore the use of reason.

Emotivism

Emotivists, on the other hand, argue that ethical words and sentences merely express people's attitudes and feelings, generating possibly different feelings and attitudes in others. For example, a pacifist and a politician are in debate. The pacifist says, 'All war is murder.' The politician argues, 'Sometimes the only way to overcome an evil dictator is to wage war.' The emotivist suggests that the debate may be characterized as follows:

Pacifist: 'War – Boo!'
Politician: 'War – Hurray!'

Moral statements are really expressions of a person's *preferences* or *emotions*: to say that something is right is really just another way of saying that one approves of it. They express the feelings of the speaker, and intend to influence the feelings of the hearer. Such statements by the politician

and the pacifist, to the emotivist, do not state any facts at all.

The fullest exploration of **emotivism** was undertaken by an American professor, Charles Stevenson (1908–79) in *Ethics and Language* (1944). Stevenson makes a distinction between conflicts of *beliefs* and conflicts of *attitude*, arguing that many disagreements about what we ought to do, about what is good or right, are not moral disagreements at all. One doctor says, 'We ought to operate', and the other says, 'No, we ought to try antibiotics'. Both doctors are in complete moral agreement that the patient should be cured and only differ in *belief* about the way to cure her. Stevenson believed that disagreements about what is right are in fact disagreements in belief. To say that something is right is really just another way of saying that 'I approve of it'. If individuals, for example, say 'Abortion is wrong', all that they are doing, according to emotivism, is announcing how they *feel* about abortion. Even if they give reasons why they believe abortion is wrong, these reasons merely appeal to emotions to support the original statement.

Critics of emotivism ask if it is a moral theory at all. If all behaviour is just about how we *feel*, how can we *know* anything? Can we not prove in some rational way that telling the truth is morally preferable to lying; that caring for animals is morally more justifiable than abusing them; that being loyal to partners is more acceptable than betrayal?

As an ethical theory emotivism undoubtedly fails because it does not take into account the connections between moral judgements and reasons. For an emotivist a moral judgement is like a command – it is chiefly a verbal means of trying to *influence* other people's attitudes and behaviour. For example, imagine that I am trying to convince you that a certain politician is evil, but you disagree. Knowing that you are a communist, I tell you that the politician in question is a fascist. This does the trick. Your attitude towards him changes and you agree that he is evil.

It would seem then that for the emotivist the fact that the politician is a fascist is a reason to agree with my judgement that he is evil. However, not any fact can count as a reason in support of any judgement. Although our values are usually little more than the expression of our **subjective** feelings, *moral judgements can ultimately only be true if backed by reasons*. In considering questions of morality, one must ask *why* a moral judgement should or should not be accepted. One might have strong feelings and might choose to ignore reason, but by doing this one is opting out of moral thinking. Moral thinking is about weighing up reasons. By focusing only on feelings, emotivism as an ethical theory fails.

The philosopher Richard Hare (b. 1919) challenged the potential reductivism of emotivism. He argued that we are too complex and diverse to reduce all our language about good, right, bad, wrong, to such a simplistic analysis. Whereas the emotivist asks what sort of effect a moral statement aims to have, Hare, a prescriptivist, *is more concerned about what is happening when somebody makes a moral statement*. In *The Language of Morals* (1952), he claimed that a moral statement such as 'Murder is wrong' is not simply an expression of feeling (as emotivists would have us believe), but rather, it is more like a *recommendation* or a *rule* such as 'Thou shalt not kill'. For Hare such statements as these are evaluative, designed to prescribe behaviour. They move beyond our specific or individual viewpoint and can be *universalized* because they are not only good for the individual but are good for everyone. As well as trying to reintroduce meaning into ethical discourse Hare also stresses the role of the imagination and the importance of **empathy** in ethics.

INTUITIONISM

ETWEEN the 1860s and the 1920s the term **intuitionism** was used for the view that there are a large number of different moral principles which cannot be put into any general order of importance in a way that would help to resolve conflicts between them. Pluralism of this sort can be contrasted with theories like utilitarianism (see pages 49–55) which hold that there is only one Supreme Principle. Today, however, an intuitionist is thought of as someone who holds a particular view about the way in which we come to find out which actions are right and which are wrong. Intuitionists in this sense claim that we grasp basic moral principles by *intuition*; moral principles are capable of being true and known through a special faculty called 'moral intuition'.

Two philosophers in the 1930s, W. D. Ross and H. A. Pritchard, claimed that there are 'facts' about what is morally right and wrong and that our understanding of these facts is sufficient enough to deserve the title 'knowledge'. We know that something is good by *intuition*: it is self-evident. You can define an action as being right if it leads to a good result. You can argue rationally about many moral problems, deciding which choices will lead to the good, but you cannot define that basic idea itself.

The major objection to intuitionism is that if what is good or what is my duty is self-evident, how can I still find myself full of doubts about the best way to proceed? Life is seldom straightforward and sometimes I might not know what to do. If people were always absolutely sure about what they should do there would be no ethical debate at all. Ross, in defence of intuitionism, argued that I know what my duty is, but this sometimes conflicts with other duties and a choice has to be made. Ethical dilemmas are therefore the result of such conflicting duties.

However, we do not always intuitively know what is the right thing to do. In a pluralistic society with different belief systems and no one single ethical tradition people may not have a clear intuition about ethics. Ethical dilemmas are contentious and open to argument and debate. Many thinkers argue that moral attitudes are not true or false but are expressions of the individual's moral position, and as such can be sincere or insincere in themselves, and consistent or inconsistent with others, but hardly mistaken or correct. If moral attitudes cannot be true or false, we should not claim that any such attitude amounts to knowledge, since knowledge is only of what is true. So on this view moral principles can be neither true nor known.

Intuitionists' claims that 'moral facts' are known by intuition seem to suggest that we have a moral faculty which reveals moral truth to us in much the same sort of way that our eyes reveal truths about our surroundings. Such a view might tempt us to accuse those who disagree with us to be morally blind; their moral faculty is not in as good working order as our own. But, in the absence of any account of how this faculty is supposed to work it became common for philosophers to complain that talk of 'moral intuition' was just an attempt to award an authority to one's own moral opinion that one was not willing to grant to others. In *After Virtue* (1981) the moral philosopher Alasdair MacIntyre had this to say about intuitionism:

Twentieth century moral philosophers have sometimes appealed to their and our intuitions, but one of the things that we ought to have learned from the history of moral philosophy is that the introduction of the word 'intuition' by a moral philosopher is always a signal that something has gone badly wrong with an argument.

HOW FREE AM I?

Your destiny shall not be allotted to you, but you shall choose it for yourselves. Let him who draws the first lot be the first to choose a life, which shall be his irrevocably. Virtue owns no master; he who honours her shall have more of her, and he who slights her less.

Plato, *Republic*

You know the alternative: either we are not free and God the all-powerful is responsible for evil. Or we are free and responsible. All the scholastic subtleties have neither added anything to nor subtracted anything from the acuteness of this paradox.

Albert Camus, *The Myth of Sisyphus* (1942)

We who lived in the concentration camps can remember the men who walked through the huts comforting others, giving away their last piece of bread. They may have been few in number but they offer sufficient proof that everything can be taken from a man but one thing: the last of the human freedoms – to choose one's attitude in any given circumstances, to choose one's own way.

Victor Frankl, *Man's Search for Meaning* (1959)

Determinism asserts that all events are totally predetermined by other events, and that freedom of choice is an illusion. We are slaves to past causes and, ultimately, have no control over our actions. Is my voluntary action at any moment completely determined by (a) my character as it has been partly inherited, partly formed by my own past actions and feelings, and/or (b) my circumstances and the external influences acting on me at that moment? Or not? Could the action I am just about to do be calculated by someone who knows my character and the forces acting upon me? Or is there a strictly incalculable element in it?

For two hundred years up to 1900 science maintained a rigid determinism and a belief in universal causation, which rejected **free will** as it rejected miracles. It saw all observable events as being subject to scientific law and, therefore, completely predictable. Scientists argued that it is ridiculous to think that the behaviour of a single species on a tiny planet in one among countless solar systems should escape a type of determinism that they observed on the widest scale of stellar magnitude and in the smallest micro-organisms.

However, from the 1850s onwards Charles Darwin (1809–82) in biology, Karl Marx (1818–83) in sociology, Sigmund Freud (1865–1939) and Ivan Pavlov (1849–1936) in psychology, all began advancing causal explanations of life, leading many people to question traditional Christian ideas that had dominated western thinking about the purpose and meaning of life.

ETHICS IN THE NINETEENTH AND TWENTIETH CENTURIES

Humanism

Humanists believe that it is possible to have a 'secular morality' – a system of values and prescriptions which can be made and maintained without reference to a God or a Moral Governor. They believe in an approach to life based on reason and our common humanity, recognizing that morality is founded on human nature and experience alone. This life is 'all we have', and it is up to us to make the best of it for ourselves and for others. Humanists do not believe in a Supreme Law-giver, but think that morality comes from human nature itself, from life experience, from empirical facts, evidence and human reason. Any ethical decision must include consideration for the well-being of those people and animals involved in a particular situation, and the wider implications of an action for future generations and the environment. Human beings, they argue, should be free from the controlling power of religious or political authority, and all of us, especially those in power, have a **responsibility** to work for the benefit of all life-forms on Earth.

For humanists, ethics and religion are not intrinsically related: *ethics is based on reason and not revelation from God.* Human beings have the ability to choose rationally, and religion is wrong to teach that people *should* behave in a certain way because if they do not, they will be punished. This sort of view, they argue, diminishes and undermines a person's freedom. What is the point of human beings having reason if all they must do at the end of the day is blindly obey some Supreme Moral Governor? Often, particularly in western culture, religion has been closely connected with morality (see page 18) with the general assumption that you cannot be a really 'good' person unless you are religious. Humanists absolutely reject this viewpoint and argue that *a person can be moral without being in any way religious.* They would argue that sometimes religious belief can lead to fanaticism and extremism which undermines human reason and makes people behave in the most violent manner. We only have to look at the Inquisition, the Crusades (see page 128) or religious sectarianism in Northern Ireland to see the strength of this argument.

Humanists would also ask a fundamental question concerning free will: if a person subscribes to theism (belief in God), then do they believe that God already knows what a person will choose to do before they themselves choose it? If God is omnipotent (all-powerful) he should be able to prevent a person doing what is wrong. If he fails to do so, he is responsible for the consequences of a person's action, aiding and abetting him or her through divine negligence, in which case a person loses moral responsibility.

Marxism and Post-Marxism

Karl Marx argued that morality is simply ideology in disguise and that it exists to serve the interests of the ruling class. Underlying society's beliefs about everything is one thing: economics. Basically, capitalism has survived so successfully because the dominant class has monopolized education, religion, the law, and ideas about morality. Belief in the disinterested nature of bourgeois 'justice' and 'morality' is just 'false consciousness', according to Marx. Only after a revolution, when everyone is free of illusions about an imposed morality, will it be possible to create a society which is free and just. Post-Marxists like Herbert Marcuse (1898–1979) and Michel Foucault (1926–84) have examined further how the spectacle of consumerism hypnotizes us into accepting the 'morality' of capitalism, consumerism and the power of multinational corporations.

Existentialism

The existentialist French philosopher Jean Paul Sartre (1905–80) believed that every individual is unique, so no one can generalize about 'human nature'. He believed that it is we ourselves who are responsible for our essential natures or characters. We are free to 'make' ourselves and if we deny this freedom we are 'inauthentic' cowards, exhibiting 'bad faith'. When people are guilty of bad faith they are guilty of not being true to themselves. They have committed the dreadful crime of denying their individuality and unique personal freedom by burying this in the 'roles' they play.

Sartre argued that we have the capacity for free and autonomous choice, and are able to *create* ourselves – not according to any set patterns, but *uniquely*, for ourselves and in ourselves. Morality comes down to the business of making 'fundamental choices'. There are no moral systems or rules or gurus that can help us. As individuals, we are totally responsible for our final decisions, including all the anguish and pain that may result from getting it wrong. We must strive to live an authentic life.

Søren Kierkegaard (1813–55), a Danish philosopher considered to be the father of existentialism, was scathing of 'part-time' Christians who go to church on Sundays but are proud, arrogant, vain and greedy on Monday. He believed that the authentic life begins with inner sincerity.

Freudianism

Until Sigmund Freud started delving into the unconscious, most moral philosophers assumed that we are always in control of our thought processes and that the choices we make are ours. According to Freud, human beings are programmed by instinctive psychic structures in layers of the unconscious which exert powerful pressures upon us to fulfil our basic desires. The super-ego, part of the unconscious mind which has internalized societal and parental taboos, is similar to the authoritarian conscience (see pages 28–9). It is like an inner voice reminding us of the social norms acquired through childhood. Being moral may not accord with our real natures at all, and so to base a moral system on what we essentially are is impossible.

Freud's most radical modern disciple, Jacques Lacan (1901–81), went even further, saying that the self itself is a fiction. It is a linguistic construct, and since language exists as a structure before the individual enters into it, then the whole notion of human identity is untenable. So self-knowledge or moral choices cannot be 'ours'.

Post-Modernism

Post-Modernism is sceptical about the existence of some kind of **objective** reality like God, or the possibility of using reason to understand it. There is no supreme principle that can tell us which ethical system is the best or truest one: we live in a relativistic universe where there are only human truths and human ethics. Lack of moral certainty makes it impossible to condemn societies whose moral belief systems we find totally repugnant.

The English philosopher A. J. Ayer (1910–89) claimed that moral language is actually meaningless. A statement such as 'murder is wrong' is simply someone expressing a feeling. This is called emotivism or 'hurray–boo theory' (see pages 7–8).

More recent Post-Modernist thinkers like Jean François Lyotard (b. 1924) and Jacques Derrida (b. 1930) claim that reason is itself a fiction, because it is a human, linguistic construct, not a transcendent entity. Our worship of reason has been the cause of much human suffering and led to dangerous political certainties which insist on 'the other'. The damage done by this 'modernism' of large totalitarian regimes holding on to the objectivity of their utopian visions is stressed by modern philosophers. In a post-modern world we are free to shop around for any set of moral values we feel are appropriate, but there are no signposts: we each have to decide for ourselves.

Female ethics

The idea that virtue is in some way gendered and that the standards and criteria of morality are different for women and men has existed in western thinking for a long time. The dominant patriarchal view has maintained that by 'nature' women are more intuitive, irrational, gentle, passive, selfless and sympathetic than men.

Early feminist Mary Wollstonecraft (1759–97) attacked this view of female 'nature' as an ideological construct whose primary function was to legitimize male supremacy in public life and to restrict women to the domestic sphere. More recently, contemporary thinkers such as feminist psychologist Carol Gilligan (b. 1936) have revived ideas of ethics being gendered. She argues that women's moral responses to problems are 'essentially' different, more cooperative and less aggressive. Such a belief is problematic if one believes, as many feminists do, that the idea of 'female nature' is a social and historical construct.

Some feminist thinkers like Martha Nussbaum (b. 1947) argue that it is men who like to invent elaborate, clinical and complex abstract formal 'systems' which they impose on the world with its moral problems. She asks whether there are specific female 'virtues' and questions the predominant patriarchal view that women 'are more intuitive, irrational, gentle, passive, selfless and sympathetic than men', and argues that these so-called 'virtues' have suppressed and restricted women.

While some feminists reject the view of female 'nature', others argue that it is irrelevant whether female virtues are innate or conditioned, and that some of the traditional 'female virtues' of cooperation and caring that operate in the private spheres of life should also be given a much higher priority in the macho and ruthless culture of the 'public sphere'.

The reality in the past has been that moral doctrines and systems have emerged from societies in which women's role has been a subordinate one. If the concerns, activities and interests traditionally associated with women were given a superior status to those traditionally associated with men, then moral priorities might become very different.

Christian feminists have urged a rethink of 'God-talk' – we are so used to hearing about God as if God were male that we do not even notice the absence of female imagery. Feminism challenges the patriarchal world view which is hierarchical, and looks to the 'inclusive' language of motherhood as well as fatherhood to express the fullness of divine love.

Gandhi

Mahatma Gandhi (1869–1948) and his ideas have had a huge impact round the world (see pages 127–8). Gandhi led the struggle for Indian independence from Britain by advocating *satyagraha*, non-violent non-cooperation. He was imprisoned several times by the British authorities and was assassinated by a Hindu nationalist in the violence that followed the partition of British India into India and Pakistan.

Satyagraha has been adopted by many campaigning groups since Gandhi's death, including the anti-nuclear arms protestors at Greenham Common, and the Newbury by-pass protestors. Gandhi once said:

All life entails violence ... Our duty can only be to minimize that which we personally exert.

Virtue theory

An influential British philosopher, Alasdair MacIntyre (b. 1929), has argued that ethics should concentrate less on private moral decisions and more on the community and its moral welfare. MacIntyre examined the beliefs of the ancient Greeks concerning the virtues – which were necessary if one wished to become a successful human being, arguing that this kind of ethical explanation has been overlooked by modern western philosophy. He felt that Kant (see pages 42–7) made morality a cold and unsympathetic exercise in reason, while the utilitarians (see pages 49–55) reduced it to a set of pseudo-scientific calculations that do not work. MacIntyre believes that these approaches have led to a moral vacuum, in which society is confused. He argues that we need to reassert Aristotle's moral and intellectual virtues in medicine, education, politics and commerce. In his book, *After Virtue* (1981), MacIntyre identifies three archetypal characters that have evolved in a **secular** society devoid of virtue:

a 'The Rich Aesthete' (Fig. 1.2), who pursues greater and 'more exciting' pleasures – the image of the ageing rock star fits this bill. Society is obsessed with these people living out their hollow fantasies for the rest of us who are led to believe by the celebrity-obsessed media that by comparison our lives are mundane and boring.

Fig. 1.2 'The Rich Aesthete'

Fig. 1.3 'The Bureaucratic Manager'

b 'The Bureaucratic Manager' (Fig. 1.3), who matches ends to means in the most efficient manner. His area of expertise is efficient management, which for him has no moral dimensions. Profit not principle rules.

c 'The Therapist', who keeps the whole show on the road, charging the rich huge amounts of money to listen to their neuroses and self-justification, which merely reflect the hollowness of their self-centred lives.

Social ethics and social contract theory

The basic idea of **social contract** theory is that morality arises from an agreement or contract made by people so that they can live together in harmony. In his book, *Leviathan* (1651), the British philosopher Thomas Hobbes (1588–1679) argues that people living in a state of nature apart from society would find life 'solitary, poor, nasty, brutish, and short'. To avoid such a life, people live together in a society. But social life is possible only if people agree to follow moral rules such as 'Don't murder', 'Don't steal', and so on.

Another philosopher who is associated with this theory is Jean-Jacques Rousseau (1712–78). In *The Social Contract* (1762) Rousseau asserts that humans living in a state of nature are 'noble savages' and it is only when they live together that they are able to reach their full potential as emotionally intelligent beings.

The British philosopher John Locke (1632–1704) made an important contribution to social contract theory in *Two Treatises of Government*, arguing that in nature humans are free and equal, but this does not mean that they can do anything they want. There is a Law of Nature, established by a Higher Consciousness, which gives each person certain natural **rights**. There is a right to life, a right to liberty, and a right to property, but to enjoy these rights, human beings must live together under a *social contract* which establishes a democratically elected government to protect their rights and to settle disputes.

Contemporary thinkers such as John Rawls (b. 1921) argue that ethics are about working out what agreements are needed to produce a *just* society. In *Theory of Justice* he asks what are the minimum requirements which ensure a balance between the needs of the individual and society. Liberty and acceptance of differences are important, he asserts; so is basic protection against poverty. Some people will inevitably do well, others less so, but all should be guaranteed a minimum standard of living, with a minimum wage. Central to the proper sense of justice is the idea that the existence of unequal possessions and distribution of such desired qualities as power, wealth and income are impermissible in today's Global Village unless these inequalities actually work to the absolute benefit of the worst-off members of the human family.

For discussion

Ideas are the most powerful things on earth.
John Maynard Keynes, economist

THE GLOBAL VILLAGE ▬

VERY day on television we witness the spectacles of violence that are taking place around the globe. Is this a worldwide upheaval or just a series of bushfires that can be extinguished one after another? Are we in a state of transition? If so, a transition from what to what? The world is always in transition. We are always passing from one phase to another. It has been said that the present does not exist. It is a small point which is overwhelmed by the shadows of the past and the ghosts of the future.

In the western world we have long believed that human beings are the masters of nature. There have also been those who believe that God rather than man is the master of the world. Whichever, we have had this illusion that we can master the natural world and also the economic and social world. But we cannot. There are real limits within which we must operate. We sometimes get answers wrong. New factors often complicate existing solutions. Solutions themselves have consequences that cannot be predicted. Paul-Marc Henry, an expert in global issues, pinpoints six modern-day problems likely to get worse, at least in the near future:

- *The population explosion.* Soon more than 60% of the world's population will be less than 25 years old. They will need jobs. But where will the jobs come from? In Europe there is already 10–12% unemployment, in Algeria 40%. We also face a world with ever-growing numbers of old people. An exploding population will affect not just economics. Much of the growth of political Islam can be explained by unemployment among young people.
- *The media.* Advertising and the media (see pages 114–15) encourage people to aspire to more. This breeds dissatisfaction. The fashion industry, too, is involved in some of the most exploitative labour conditions in the world: Michael Jordan earned US $20 million for endorsing Nike shoes – more than Nike's 30,000-strong Indonesian workforce earned making them; Disney Corporation's *Pocahontas* shirts sell at US $10.97 each and are made by workers

in Haiti earning just US $10.77 a week for making thousands of shirts every week.

- *Distribution of resources.* It may not be possible for western countries to maintain existing levels of protection for the aged and the weak. The great achievement of western civilization in the twentieth century – the improvement of basic income and a social security net – may now be in danger. Increasingly, people are asking questions about taxation systems. Should people have the right to refuse to pay taxes to maintain armed forces if they are pacifists (see pages 119–21)? Should the rich be taxed more than they are, to help pay for the National Health Service? Is it morally permissible that a footballer or company director can earn more in a week than a nurse can earn in a year?

- *Migration.* In the next twenty years every country on Earth will feel the effect of mass movements of people whose only hope of improvement is migration.

- *Deterioration.* Our existing social and economic infrastructure is deteriorating. Technology, rather than easing the problem, actually creates unemployment.

- *Natural Resources.* These are running out: by 2020 the consumption of energy in the world will increase by more than 50%. We now have 500 million cars and by then there will be one billion cars. Most of the increase will occur in Asia.

All the leaders of the world's faiths believe that politicians must begin to sacrifice short-term interests for the sake of future generations, arguing that the principle of responsibility is not being taken seriously enough by decision-makers. We are living through a second technological revolution aggravated by a population explosion. It is irresponsible, they say, to spend trillions of dollars on weapons of mass destruction when a redistribution of wealth is needed for projects such as rebuilding the transportation system between north and south Africa, which would cost in comparison only US $30 billion and improve the quality of life for a whole continent

> *The uniqueness of the spiritual dimension is that it gives a reason for the absoluteness and universality of ethical obligations ... an unconditional claim, a 'categorical' ought, cannot be derived from the finite dimension of human existence.*
> Hans Küng, *Catholic theologian*

The Internet, mass communications, shorter travelling times, satellite TV, all make the world a 'smaller' place – and Hindus can learn from Christians who in turn can learn from Muslims who can learn from Buddhists and so on.

INTER-RELIGIOUS DIALOGUE

MANY of the ethical arguments discussed in this book are couched within ideas that have been promoted by the Christian religion. This does not mean that all the thinkers and philosophers studied in this book are Christians, but illustrates that the examination syllabuses, set in a western culture, are influenced by Christian ideas because they pervade much of western European thinking. The same could be said of people living within predominantly Muslim, Hindu, Sikh or Buddhist traditions. The views people have about the meaning and value of life reflect their cultural or religious background. It must also be noted that while religions have teachings common to each other, practices may differ (for example, Buddhists may not eat meat, Hindus refrain from eating cows, and Muslims and Jews from eating pork).

Although all the world religions have taught the way of peace, there has often been a tragic complicity between conflict and religion, which has often spilled out into open warfare on the battlefield. Religious fanaticism still fuels conflicts in the world today. Over recent decades there has been a growing consciousness that there will be no world peace until there is peace between

Fig. 1.5 A Muslim girl in prayer. All the world religions teach that ethics and religion are one and the same

the world religions. Dialogue has been particularly successful in the exploration of the ethical dimension of the world religions, which all share:

- a conviction that the human family is one
- the view that belief and ethical behaviour are both one and the same, yet relate to the Absolute – 'Love your neighbour by loving God'
- a sense of the sacredness and dignity of all life forms
- a belief in the human community living according to egalitarian principles
- a recognition that might is not right and that human power is not sufficient or absolute
- a vision that **compassion** and the force of inner truthfulness have greater power than hate or self-interest
- a feeling of obligation to stand on the side of the poor and the oppressed
- a hope that good will finally prevail.

EXAM QUESTIONS

1 Discuss the impact of the feminist movement on the role of women in society. [Oxford and Cambridge, 1998]

2 What justification is there for the humanist insistence that moral behaviour has nothing to do with belief in God? [EDEXCEL, 1997]

3 Compare and contrast religious views of human purpose and fulfilment with either existentialist views or humanist views. [NEAB, 1997]

4 'Religious ethics are superior to secular ethics.' Discuss. [EDEXCEL, 1998]

5 How valuable are intuition and emotion as sources of moral authority? [EDEXCEL, 1997]

6 Study the passage below and then answer the questions which follow.

Instead of taking up practical issues, moral philosophers limited themselves to the study of the nature of morality, or (in the heyday of linguistic philosophy) to the study of the meaning of moral judgements. This came to be known as 'meta-ethics' a term which signified that they were not actually taking part in ethics, but were engaged in a high-level study about ethics. Normative ethics, the study of general theories about what is good and bad, right and wrong, was considered an important part of ethics until the 1930s. Then it too was relegated to a secondary concern, except for occasional discussions of utilitarianism and the different forms it might take.

Source: Singer, P. '*Applied Ethics*', UP (1986), p.2.

a What are the distinguishing features of 'moral judgements'?

b Comment on the distinction between 'meta-ethics' and ethics.

c Evaluate the views of at least *two* philosophers on the meaning of 'good'.

[EDEXCEL, 1995]

2 Ethics and religion

ETHICS BEFORE THE GREEKS

BECAUSE we are brought up in a western society, it sometimes seems as though philosophy, science and ethics were unknown before the Classical period in Greece, around the fifth to third centuries BCE. In fact, everything that was necessary for civilization had been developed thousands of years before the Greeks by the ancient civilizations of Iraq, India, Egypt and China. Irrigation, agriculture, stock-breeding, pottery, weaving, architecture, mining, metalwork, ocean-going ships, writing, painting, sculpture, poetry, dance and the martial arts, mathematics, astronomy, surveying, philosophy, science and medicine had all been employed for thousands of years. The ancient world did not develop ethics as we know it, as its approach to ethics was *prescriptive* (see pages 4–5).

For the great civilizations of Egypt and India, the existence of God and the divine world was almost unquestioned, and the after-death fate of human beings was decided by the purity and goodness of their conduct during this life. For the people of Egypt, always known as deeply religious, the supreme truth was the principle of Maat, the divine order of justice which underlies the visible universe. The role of individuals was to purify themselves and serve the divine in this life so that after death they might live with God in an astral heaven for all eternity: after judgement the evil would be destroyed in the underworld while the good attained an immortal body.

In India this principle of universal moral order, called **dharma**, is to be found in the operation of natural law and in the laws of morality. According to Indian thought, *all actions have consequences*. As we sow, so shall we reap, and the fruits of actions are like their seed: if we act with harmful or selfish intent, then not only will other people be hurt, but we also will suffer in the long run. If we act with benevolent intent, not only will others be helped, but our actions will purify our hearts and bring us closer to God.

Indian philosophy sees Brahman, the Universal Godhead, as the Ground of Being, without form, unconditioned, unborn, beyond death, time and space. This is the one Being, the only thing that can truly be said to exist, and all beings are like sparks of this spiritual fire. All things are interrelated, mutually dependent and arising together. As Universal Consciousness, the light of awareness appears in all things, veiled by the darkness of this world. Our task is to penetrate through the darkness of Maya, the magical illusion of God's play, to escape from the bondage of our desires and to achieve enlightenment. Three snares hold us fast to this world – greed, anger and lust – and it is by overcoming and rejecting these that we

Fig. 2.1 Hindu Swami

can find the universal light in our own hearts. What keeps human beings in ignorance and suffering is their sense of separateness – their **egoism** – and by overcoming the illusion of separateness they can know their real self, a manifestation of the Universal Being.

The great spiritual teachers of India such as Krishna, Buddha and Guru Nanak taught a path to salvation through meditation and prayer, through good thoughts and kind acts; and the beginning of the path was found in ethical conduct. Virtues like truthfulness, non-stealing, non-violence and compassion are prescribed in order to purify the mind and make it fit for religious practice, and to bring society into harmony with the Universal Law.

The temple-schools of India, Iraq and Egypt were the source of all scientific and spiritual knowledge in the Ancient World, but depended on faith in the teachers and the teaching – there was little room for questioning or disbelief. Religious faith was easier in the Ancient World when living prophets experienced God and taught the truths of His revelation, but by the Classical era it seemed as if the gods no longer spoke to humankind. Moses saw God face to face, but by the time of the second temple (around 500 BCE) God was silent; in Greece the gods of Mount Olympus no longer spoke to the people and so philosophers began to question religious belief itself. If the gods did not exist, or were so capricious as not to be trusted, then human beings were alone in the universe and had to work out their own salvation.

In the ancient world suffering was from God, and a necessary part of our purification from the effects of our past actions; what was 'good' was what brought us closer to God, even if that meant losing everything we hold dear in this world; what was 'evil' was what separated us from God. *In the Classical world people began to think that what was good was what was pleasant and what was painful was evil, and this is an attitude which has remained to this day in the assumptions of our society.* But from the point of view of Indian philosophy this view is deeply mistaken, for we have

identified with an illusion, the notion of a separate personality which experiences pain and pleasure. The illusion is that we think we can achieve lasting satisfaction through pleasure, wealth and power, whereas the only lasting satisfaction comes from waking up to our true condition and becoming free beings.

THE GREEKS

EVER since people have lived together in groups they have found it necessary to regulate behaviour in order to ensure the group's well-being. Pythagoras (c. 580–500 BCE) (Fig. 2.2) taught that the intellectual nature was superior to the sensual nature and founded a semi-religious order with rules regulating behaviour and rituals that demonstrated ethical beliefs. Pythagoreans taught a sharp dualism between mortal human bodies and immortal human souls. They believed in the

Fig. 2.2 Pythagoras

fundamental unity of all life and individual souls as fragments of the divine, universal soul. The aim of human existence was spiritual purity – silence, contemplation and abstention from animal flesh – which prepared the soul for its return to the divine soul. The soul is imprisoned in the material world, and at death will be reborn into a new body – human or animal. Pythagorean ideas influenced later Greek thought: the immortality of the soul; the existence of Universals in a world of higher Truth; and reason and philosophy as means by which humans can reach the divine.

One of the most impressive examples of group living was the Greek State or *Polis* of Athens in the fifth century BCE with a population of around 250,000. The Greeks developed a democratic state, governed by commonly agreed laws. Although women and slaves had no political power, and the rich and powerful became the policy-makers, the Athenians developed ideas such as the right to vote, fair trials, democracy, and philosophical thinking. The Greeks speculated freely about the nature of the world and the meaning of life without being fettered by any inherited orthodoxy.

In the fifth century BCE the Sophists taught that all human judgement is subjective and we can never fully understand objective values. Socrates (c. 470–399 BCE) disagreed, and his ideas are represented in the dialogues of his pupil Plato (c. 428–c. 347 BCE), who argued that **virtue** is knowledge, people will be virtuous if they know what virtue is, and that evil or vice is the result of ignorance. Socrates believed that if people are educated about what constitutes virtue they will become moral.

Some of his ideas challenged the conventional norms of Athens of the time, particularly his view that it is better to be wronged than to wrong someone else. Perhaps most strange to the ears of the Athenian rulers was his vision of a state ruled *not by politicians but by philosophers*, an idea which still challenges the political status quo today. Socrates argued his ideas in the public places of Athens in a process in which people discussed ideas openly. Perhaps surprisingly, he declared that as for himself he 'knew nothing' and was only wise because he knew that he knew nothing. Despite this, he believed that knowledge was obtainable and that the search for knowledge and understanding was the highest and noblest of all pursuits.

By using questions and answers, known as 'the dialectic method', Socrates and his followers pursued knowledge. Socrates argued that individual life had a purpose (*teleos*). He believed that we have a 'real self' inside us – something essential that is truly and deeply 'I'. Morality, treating others well, is the key to Truth. Although moral knowledge is attainable through discussion, Socrates stressed that morality is not the sort of knowledge that can actually be taught. Real knowledge is about 'essences' of things like 'Justice' that all individuals have to discover for themselves in everyday life experiences.

Most later Greek schools of moral philosophy were derived from Socrates' teachings. These included the following:

- The Cynics believed that pleasure was evil, and pride, including pride in appearance, was a vice, leading them to look wild and prompting Socrates to say to one of them, 'I can see your pride through the holes in your cloak'. The Cyrenaics and Hedonists (see pages 50–1) argued that pleasure was the chief good (as long as one does not become obsessed by it).
- Plato, in the *Republic*, his greatest work, argued that good is the essential element of reality. Evil does not exist. It is merely an imperfect reflection of the real, which is good. In *Dialogues* he argues that human virtue lies in our ability to perform our proper *function* in the world. The human soul has three elements, each possessing a specific virtue:
  - Intellect: the virtue of intellect is wisdom and understanding about the meaning of life.

– Will: the virtue of will is courage: the capacity to act and to be.
– Emotion: the virtue of emotion is self-control in speech, and behaviour.

For Plato the ultimate virtue is Justice, a sublime state which sees the three elements of the soul working together in harmony: the intellect sovereign, followed by the will and then the emotions. The 'Just' person is someone whose life is balanced in this way.

- Stoicism later taught that nature is rational and ordered, and only a life led in harmony with nature can be good. By practising the virtues of courage, practical wisdom and justice, we can attain *apatheia* – peace, well-being and a detachment from external events. Epicureanism, founded by Epicurus (341–270 BCE), taught that to achieve the 'highest good', which it identified as pleasure, individuals must be self-disciplined, serene, able to eliminate emotional disturbance and postpone immediate pleasure if they wish to attain more secure and lasting satisfaction in the future.

- Aristotle (384–322 BCE), philosopher, scientist and pupil of Plato, taught that the aim of life was the attainment of happiness (*eudaimonia*). Aristotle taught that happiness can be achieved in a number of ways and in *Nicomachean Ethics* analyses character and intelligence as they relate to happiness. A moral virtue is always the mean, a middle way between excess and deficiency (the Golden Mean). He distinguishes two types of virtue or human excellence:
  – moral virtues or qualities of character (such as courage, liberality, temperance, modesty) – *cultivated through habit*
  – intellectual virtues or qualities of mind (such as wisdom, understanding and judgement) – *cultivated through instruction.*

There is more to morality than doing what is good or right. If I decide not to drink and drive because I might get caught, my decision is borne out of *prudential* reasons (I'm careful to consider the advantages by avoiding risks), rather than ethical ones. If we are to be sincere about ethics, we have to acknowledge that *motives* and *intentions* as well as actions are morally significant.

For discussion

Read the virtues below and then, without looking at the book, write down (a) the excesses and (b) the deficiencies of each virtue. Discuss your findings.

Excess	Virtue	Deficiency
rashness	*courage*	cowardice
licentiousness	*temperance*	insensibility
prodigality	*liberality*	illiberality
vulgarity	*magnificence*	pettiness
vanity	*magnanimity*	pusillanimity
ambition	*proper ambition*	unambitiousness
irascibility	*patience*	lack of spirit
boastfulness	*truthfulness*	understatement
buffoonery	*wittiness*	boorishness
obsequiousness	*friendliness*	cantankerousness
shyness	*modesty*	shamelessness
envy	*righteous indignation*	malicious enjoyment

Even more than our actions they reflect the kind of people we are, our inner character.

Virtue ethics look at character and from what we do *outwardly* to the kind of persons we are *inwardly*. Aristotle's ethics are called virtue ethics because the virtues or qualities of character are at the heart of his arguments.

THE MEANING OF 'GOOD' ■

AN important word that is commonly used in ethics and religion is 'Good'. For Aristotle 'Good' is defined as something which fulfils its own particular *function*. On this theory, a 'good' pen is one that writes well; a 'good' guitar is one that plays well. This view formed the basis of what is called the Natural Law approach to ethics (see pages 26–7) – morality is embodied in Nature which contains 'natural laws' which human beings must follow to fulfil this law which is 'Good'.

A Christian may believe that good is what God approves of and that the Bible acts as a guide in influencing the individual in what actions and thoughts are good. A Buddhist may believe that good is that which brings peace, repose and understanding, thus living in accord with the Laws of the Universe. The meaning of the words 'good' and 'happiness' for particular individuals depends then on different background, beliefs and experiences, and sometimes there will be agreement and sometimes there will be disagreement.

To be moral, then, according to Natural Law, has to do with the *function* of a human being. But what is my function? Why am I here? What must I do? Who am I? Anything that is good or bad is so because it *functions* well or badly; and if we could discover the function of human beings we would understand how the words good or bad could be applied to them. Aristotle himself arrived at the theory that the proper function of human beings is *to reason*, and that being moral was reasoning well. By reasoning well,

Aristotle argued, people would have a successful, fulfilled and harmonious life:

He who exercises his reason and cultivates it seems to be both in the best state of mind and most dear to the gods. For if the gods have any care for human affairs, as they are thought to have, it would be reasonable both that they should delight in that which was best and most akin to them (i.e. reason) and that they should reward those who love and honour this most, as caring for the things that are dear to them and acting both rightly and nobly.

Nicomachean Ethics

CHRISTIANITY ■

THE ethical systems of Greece did not extend to non-Greeks, who were called 'barbarians'; nor did it extend to slaves. The coming of Christianity, however, with its vision of moral citizenship and **equality** for all, irrespective of social position or race, appealed to the peoples of the west.

At the heart of Christian tradition are some fundamental questions: What am I worth? What is my purpose? What is my destiny? What am I called to be, as an individual and as a member of the human family? What constitutes human dignity? What are the social as well as the individual dimensions of human dignity and responsibility? How does divine forgiveness and grace engage with human frailty in the realization of human happiness? How are the conditions of human life related to the goal of human fulfilment? What are the implications of my creatureliness which I share with other animals?

Christianity, as taught by the early Church, maintained that, ultimately, a person achieves goodness only with the help of God's grace, and that human will or intelligence alone cannot achieve the *summum bonum* (the final value *desirable in itself* and not merely as a means to an end). Jesus' message of God's love, forgiveness, and mercy, relayed with such beauty and simplicity, resonated in the minds and hearts of men and women all over the ancient world.

The basic ethical belief of Jesus is stated in the **Golden Rule** (see pages 97–8) common to all the world's religions: 'So whatever you wish that men would do to you, do so to them' (Matthew 7:12); and at the heart of Christian ethics is the Sermon on the Mount (Matthew 5–7) (see pages 35–6). Jesus taught that the essence of Jewish law lies in the commandment: 'You shall love the Lord your God with all your heart, and with all your soul, and with all your strength, and with all your mind; and your neighbour as yourself' (Luke 10:27).

For discussion

Christ's commandments are not a question of ethics, they are pure pragmatism.

Peter Rogers, American artist

The early Christians believed that martyrdom, forgiveness and **agape** (the kind of unreserved love that God has for creation) were important elements of morality. Their courage, faith and decency when faced with torture and death impressed many, and when we consider the barbarism of the rulers who opposed religious freedom, it is remarkable that Christian thought not only survived but went on to influence western culture for the next 2000 years. Although Jesus' message was a peaceful one, the ensuing history of the Christian churches was often racked with cruelty, oppression, violence – the Crusades, **Islamophobia**, the Inquisition, anti-Semitism, intra-Christian rivalry.

DOES ETHICS DEPEND ON RELIGION?

H UMANISTS (see page 10) and atheists see no connection between religion and ethics, arguing that it is possible to be ethical without being religious. Popular thinking, however, understands ethics and religion as being inseparable, a view shared by Muslims, Christians, Hindus, Jews, etc. It is not unusual for religious leaders to be regarded as moral 'experts' and invited to sit on ethics committees, especially those concerned with medical ethics. Because religious leaders are the spokespeople for religion it is assumed that they must be spokespeople for morality too. In discussing the proposed connection, or lack of it, between religion and ethics, we will focus on one religion, Christianity.

GOD AS LAW-GIVER

F ROM a Christian perspective, life is created and there are higher levels of consciousness beyond the human. Christians look to a Supreme Being who is all-loving (benevolent), all-powerful (omnipotent) and all-knowing (omniscient): a Creator and Supreme Law-giver who continually brings into existence a meaningful universe. God's purpose for humankind has been revealed through the Holy Scriptures, the Church, the Prophets, and through natural reason. These sources teach that God has promulgated laws which, if followed, allow people to live in harmony with themselves and with others. In the Judaeo-Christian tradition the most famous of these laws are the Ten Commandments (see page 35).

For Judaism, Christianity and Islam, God requires something of humankind, and stands ready to reward obedience and punish violation. But what sort of God is it that creates **obligations** and commandments? Religious conviction concerning God's dealings with people affects the basic relationship of religion and ethics. God has something to do with the very meaning of obligation. Biblical writers do not view ethics *naturalistically*, i.e. rooted in human nature or in the social environment, or *abstractly* in terms of some generalizations about human values, but *theologically* as rooted in the nature and activity of God; and, as a consequence, our relation to God is thought to be of vital importance, not simply for ethics, but within ethical theory itself. Christians believe that they have obligations to the following:

- *A righteous God* – the Bible is sometimes called 'The Book of God's righteousness'. God's steadfast faithfulness to the Covenant is a recurring theme.
- *A just God* – numerous passages in the Bible refer to God as *just* (Micah 6:8).
- *A personal God* – people who fail in remaining true to God's *covenant obligations*, derive knowledge of the true meaning of human 'justice or righteousness' from God's grace (the measure of His righteousness) not from anything they themselves think or do (see Hosea, Job and Isaiah).
- *An incarnate God* – Jesus Christ is at the heart of all ethical thinking.
- *A merciful God.*

THE DIVINE COMMAND THEORY

For discussion

Is conduct right because the gods command it, or do the gods command it because it is right?

This became one of the most famous questions in the history of philosophy. The twentieth-century British philosopher Antony Flew believed that 'one good test of a person's aptitude for philosophy is to discover whether he can grasp its force and point'. See if you can grasp it by discussing it with your partner.

This theory, which has permeated traditional Christian ethics, sees an act as morally right if it has been commanded by God and morally wrong if God has forbidden it. In other words, right and wrong become an objective matter: it is right if God the Law-

giver, the Supreme Moral Governor, commands it, and wrong if God does not. Ethics, therefore, is not merely a matter of custom or personal feelings but relates to a 'Higher Good'.

In Plato's dialogue the *Euthyphro*, Socrates and Euthyphro discuss the following question which has fascinated thinkers down the ages and *still* challenges us today: 'Is conduct right because the gods command it, or do the gods command it because it is right?' (**Euthyphro's dilemma**) – a question which goes to the heart of the relationship between ethics and religion.

This question suggests that to accept the **Divine Command theory** puts us in a dilemma. If we agree that God's laws are absolute (for example the reason we must not lie is because God commands it), we have a problem. We could ask why doesn't God command laws which allow cruel actions as well as good actions? If He commanded that we lie, for example, then lying, not truthfulness, would be regarded as being acceptable behaviour. Socrates, on the other hand, argues that God commands right behaviour because it *is* right, and God's commands are the result of his omniscience and infinite wisdom. God is good, and only commands what is good. If God is good, he can only command what is right.

However, this assumes that there is a standard of goodness *independent* of God. God is no longer the ultimate standard of morality. We are saying that God sees that truthfulness is right, yet this is very different from his *making* it right. The idea of rightness exists prior to and independent of God's command. So if we want to know why we should try and be truthful the reply 'Because God commands it' will not take us very far. We can still ask 'But why does God command it?' and the answer to that question will give us the underlying reasons why truthfulness is a good thing. However, theists, who think of God as the Supreme Moral Governor, argue that God would never command anything evil because God is benevolent (all-loving). However, a father can be loving, but sometimes he might decide to 'be cruel to be kind'. Try and think of some examples! We still have the problem as to whether what is loving depends on God's will or whether there is an independent standard of what it is to be benevolent.

For discussion

Who decides what is good? If it is God, then presumably he could call lying good, and it would be. Who wants a God like that? If it is not God, since he has to obey a higher law just as we do, then he is not supreme. Who wants a God like that?

Socrates

Theists would argue that goodness is not something *external* to God, but rather something with which he is fully *identified*. Goodness is what the word God means. He could no more cease to be good than he could cease to be God. In the Hebrew Bible, for example, God is constantly celebrated in terms of loving kindness and merciful compassion. This goodness does not mean that God cannot also be just, and He is sometimes portrayed in religious literature as a fierce judge, but never inconsistent in His loving nature either: 'The Lord is just in all his ways, and kind in his doings ... Righteousness and justice are the foundation of the throne' (Psalms 145, 89).

Criticisms of the Divine Command theory

- It assumes that a God exists who issues commands. This is very difficult to prove to somebody who refuses to believe in God. The history of philosophy contains numerous attempts to prove that a personal God exists, but it is safe to say that each of these 'proofs' is controversial.
- Even assuming that God exists, there are the problems associated with human

understanding and ignorance in finding out what God's commands exactly are.
- If the Bible is the Word of God, we still have the problem of interpreting it. Different people interpret the Bible in different ways (see pages 34–5).
- Why should we obey a Supreme Moral Governor in the first place? Surely threats of reward or punishment are not good moral reasons for obedience? Don't we have a right, indeed a duty, to decide for ourselves what is right and wrong?
- It seems that no satisfactory answer can be given to the dilemma: *is an act right because God commands it, or does God command it because it is right?* If an act is right simply because God commands it, then its being right is merely arbitrary. God could arbitrarily command a person to murder his or her child (as in the Biblical story of Abraham and his son Isaac), and that would supposedly make it right. But would it? On the other hand, if God commands an act because it is right, then a standard of rightness exists independent of God's commands. It might be, say, the Principle of Utility (see pages 49–55). If so, then we could discover this principle without knowing God's commands. God's commands, therefore, are not necessarily a prerequisite for living a moral life.

Review

The various arguments about the connection between ethics and religion point to a common conclusion. Right and wrong are not to be defined in terms of God's will; morality is a matter of reason and conscience, not religious faith; and religious considerations do not always provide definite solutions to the specific moral problems that confront us. However, this conclusion does not undermine the validity of religion but illustrates that the discipline known as 'Ethics' *can* remain independent.

THE NATURAL LAW THEORY

THE term **Natural Law** usually refers to *prescriptive* moral laws that are supposed to be derived from human nature, as distinguished from *descriptive* laws of nature such as those found in chemistry and physics. Aristotle believed that everything serves a purpose. He distinguished between 'efficient causes' and 'final causes' – an efficient cause is what gets things done and the final cause is the end product. Everything, every object and every action, has some final purpose and this is what determines its good. If we understand what that good is we will know what we need to do in order to achieve it. The Christian thinkers of the Middle Ages agreed. Nature was seen as manifesting the purpose of the Creator who established order in all things. They used the expression Natural Law to refer to whatever principles are taken to govern human conduct, other than those which originate in human legislation.

St Thomas Aquinas

The Natural Law theory claims, therefore, that everything is created for a particular purpose, and fulfilling this purpose is the good to which everything aims. Its most famous exponent was St Thomas Aquinas (1225–74), regarded as the greatest of all scholastic philosophers. Aquinas developed Aristotle's ideas and argued that the world was created, and as such has God's ultimate purpose as its final end or good. According to Aquinas, human beings survive physical death and, ultimately, the purpose of human existence does not lie just in this life. However, we have been endowed with reason and freedom and can choose to follow 'natural law', the rational understanding and following of God's final purpose.

For Aquinas this *purpose* was to reproduce, to learn, to live harmoniously in society and to worship God. By using reason men and women discover God's intention and the purpose of human existence; thus arriving at the principles of Natural Law, which describes not only how things *are*, but also specify how things *ought* to be as well. Things are as they ought to be when they are fulfilling their natural purpose, and unnatural when they are not. Moral laws, therefore, have their source in Natural Law – some ways of behaving are natural but some are unnatural and therefore morally wrong. Aquinas argued that:

- human nature was created by God; and each person has a particular purpose
- there is a link between happiness and virtuous behaviour
- reason can guide people in developing virtue
- morality is not based on commands from God but on reason – 'the moral life is the life according to reason' (*Summa Theologica*)
- there is an 'ideal' human nature which we all can potentially achieve
- 'sin' is falling short of this ideal (the good), literally meaning 'missing the mark' (as in archery). People often miss the mark because they confuse apparent good with the ideal (for example, drinking alcohol may make me feel more sociable – apparent good – but the ideal would be feeling self-confident and sociable without having to chemically alter my body)
- although an act may be good in itself (for example giving to charity), it may come from a bad intention (giving to charity so you can boast about it).

Natural Law theory today

Such ideas seem reasonable enough; for example it is 'natural' for us to care about others because we are social animals. However, the application of the Natural Law theory to sexual ethics has caused controversy (Fig. 2.3). If everything has a natural purpose, then the purpose of sex is procreation (having babies). Religious thinkers have traditionally opposed sexual practices not aimed at procreation as 'deviant' or 'unnatural' – practices such as masturbation, gay sex, oral or anal sex or sex while using contraceptives – and condemned them because they are not

Fig 2.3   Gay rights protestors challenge the traditional Natural Law approach to sexual ethics

fulfilling the 'natural' purpose of sex. This way of thinking about sex dates back to St Augustine in the sixth century (see page 85) and traditionally has been the basis of moral theology. Today many of these values are questioned:

- Philosophical thinking has provoked philosophers to question a *prescriptivist approach* to ethics. The Scottish philosopher David Hume (1771–76) argued that *what is* the case and *what ought* to be the case are logically different ideas; for example, sex *does* produce babies but this does not necessarily mean that people *ought* to have sex *only* for this purpose (see pages 4–5 for more on the 'is/ought' controversy).

- Modern science has presented a world view which makes little or no reference to purposes or values. All life has its particular characteristics not because it is the way it *ought to be* but because of *the way it is*, dictated by factors like natural selection, evolution and the laws of cause and effect. 'Natural laws' are the laws of biology, chemistry and physics; morality and values have nothing to do with the natural order. (Although this viewpoint has permeated western thinking over the last two or three hundred years, modern nuclear physics is discovering that even the smallest atom is part of an intrinsically complex, law-conforming and meaningful universe.)

- Moral judgements arise from human reason which we are able to understand because God has made us rational beings. However, because the Natural Law theory sees the ultimate recourse to moral decisions and actions as reason, this means that the religious believer has no special access to moral truth. The believer and the nonbeliever are in exactly the same position. God made everyone rational, not just believers.

Review

For believers and nonbelievers alike, making a moral judgement is a matter of listening to one's reason. Even Aquinas believed that ultimately the moral life is the life 'according to reason', and in *Summa Theologica* argued that acting reasonably and acting as a Christian are the same thing:
To disparage the dictate of reason is equivalent to condemning the word of God ... Conscience is the dictate of reason ... he who acts against his conscience always sins.

But what is 'conscience'?

CONSCIENCE

Thus conscience doth make cowards of us all.

   William Shakespeare, *Hamlet* (c. 1603)

If one trains one's conscience it will kiss us as it bites.

Friedrich Nietzsche, *Beyond Good and Evil*

Do what thy manhood bids thee do,
From none but self expect applause;
He noblest lives and noblest dies
Who makes and keeps his self-made laws.

   Richard Burton, British explorer and translator of the *Arabian Nights*

There is perhaps no nobler statement than the one that goes something like: 'I shall act according to my conscience.' Throughout history people have upheld the principles of justice and peace despite every kind of pressure to relinquish what they knew and believed. The Old Testament prophets, for example, acted and spoke according to their conscience when they denounced and predicted society's collapse because of greed, ignorance and corruption. Jesus of Nazareth was sentenced to death and crucified for speaking out according to his conscience. In the bloody corridors of human history the 'small voice of conscience' has often spoken, and men and women have stood up against injustice, **prejudice** and tyranny. Without the existence of 'conscience' there is little doubt that humanity would be even more barbaric than it is today.

However, some, motivated by conscience, have actually harmed others. In fact, there is hardly any act of cruelty or indifference that has not been sanctioned by conscience; as the French philosopher Blaise Pascal (1623–62) reminds us: 'Men never do evil so fully and so happily as when they do it for conscience's sake.'

Authoritarian conscience

So what is conscience? Before looking at religious ideas, let us consider the work of Erich Fromm (1900–80), a German psycho-analyst who escaped Nazi Germany for the US when the fascists came to power in 1933. Fromm argued that we are born into a world massively influenced by external authorities – our parents, schools, churches. The laws and sanctions that these authorities put on us, says Fromm, *become part of ourselves*. Instead of feeling responsible to something outside of ourselves, we feel responsible to something inside which we call *conscience*. These laws and sanctions, which in fact come from external authority, become *internalized*. Conscience becomes, therefore, a very effective way of regulating conduct; far more effective than fear of these external authorities

regulated by fear of punishment or hope of reward. This *authoritarian conscience* is determined by the fact that its commands are pronounced by authority. People are trapped by these external authorities and their 'internalized echo'.

The presence of an external authority, of which a person is in awe, is the source which continuously feeds the internalized authority, the conscience. The contents of authoritarian conscience are derived from its commands; its strength rooted in the emotions of fear and admiration for the authority. Good conscience is consciousness of pleasing the external (and internal) authority. Guilty conscience is the consciousness of displeasing it. The good authoritarian conscience produces a feeling of well-being and security. The guilty conscience produces fear and insecurity, because acting against the will of the authority implies being punished, or worse still, being deserted by that authority. Being deserted by the authority is frightening because it means being thrown into the horror of nothingness by something felt to be more powerful and greater in all respects than oneself.

So the worst offence in the authoritarian situation is disobedience. The authority is superior to oneself – it cannot be questioned. If one tries to assert one's own will, then guilt arises. A person's own power is curbed by feelings of guilt rooted in the conviction that the exercise of one's will is a rebellion against the authority's supposed right to be the sole creator. These feelings of guilt weaken us, reduce our power and increase our submission.

Fromm argued that often we are made to feel guilty because of our strivings to be strong, proud, productive, independent – our own person. We are made to feel good from feelings of submission, obedience, dependence, powerlessness and 'sinfulness'. This might seem paradoxical but nevertheless this is the result of authoritarian conscience. The very fact of having a guilty conscience is in itself a sign of one's virtue, because a guilty conscience is the symptom of one's 'fear and trembling' before the ultimate authoritarian conscience, whether it be God or the state.

The paradoxical result is that the authoritarian guilty conscience becomes the basis for a good conscience, while the good conscience, if one should have it, ought to create feelings of guilt. So the first result of this internalization of conscience is that people submit to the external authorities. The second result can be equally negative. This is when a person takes over the role of the authority by treating herself with the same strictness and cruelty. A person becomes not only the obedient slave but also the strict taskmistress who treats herself as her own slave, imposing the commands of the external authority on to all aspects of life, condemning and judging herself if she fails.

Most religious and political systems in history serve as illustrations of the authoritarian conscience. On another level, too, the authoritarian conscience plays an enormous role in producing and sustaining the negative and destructive feelings of guilt. Parents, by their power, can make children feel guilty in a number of ways. Children feel guilty that they are not fulfilling parents' expectations, leading Fromm to conclude that *at the bottom of every neurosis is a parent.*

For discussion

In a fascist society or religion two areas of the self are aborted or forbidden to develop naturally: sexuality and aggression. Persons are not educated to be true selves but to wear false personas modelled on the demands of the parents and not on the needs of the self. The child, thus instructed, often channels these powers of sexuality and aggression into self-loathing and contempt – the original sin mentality – the notion that I came into the world despised, unwanted, ugly, and powerless. It may be displaced onto a scapegoat, for example racial minorities, women or homosexuals. It can be transformed into worship of the oppressor who is 'always right'. Finally it can be eroticized in sado-masochistic fantasies and practices.

Matthew Fox, modern theologian

Humanistic conscience

Inasmuch as parental authority, religious or social authority tends to break the child's will, spontaneity and independence, children, not being born to be broken, struggle and rebel against the authority. They fight for their freedom, not only from pressure, but also for freedom to be themselves, fully fledged human beings and not conforming 'carbon-copy replica-reacting machines'. For some children the battle for freedom will be more successful. The battle lines are marked – the children or young people who want to be themselves, against the external authorities who want them to conform to the laws and sanctions that *they* represent. Erich Fromm, however, defines humanistic conscience as real conscience – *that which judges our functions as human beings; it is the root of the word 'con-scientia' indicating knowledge within oneself, knowledge of our respective success or failure in the art of living.*

Actions, thoughts and feelings which help the proper functioning and unfolding of our total personality produce a feeling of inner approval. Actions, thoughts and feelings that produce a feeling of uneasiness are characteristic of the guilty conscience. Fromm calls humanistic conscience 'a re-action of ourselves to ourselves'. It is the voice of our *true selves* summoning us to live productively, to develop fully and harmoniously, to become what we potentially are. In true conscience, therefore, we preserve the knowledge of our aim in life and of the principles we have discovered ourselves, as well as those we have learned from others. We are able to live with integrity. Authoritarian conscience on the other hand is concerned with obedience and 'social adjustment'.

The voice of real conscience, however, cannot always be heard – the less productively one lives, the weaker becomes one's conscience. A tragic aspect of human existence is that our conscience is often weakest when we need it most and we listen to every voice but our own. We are constantly hammered by the noise of opinions, arguments, ideas from 'out there'. We live in a confusing world of chattering tongues – digital television, gossip, lyrics and sound-bites. We seldom are alone. Perhaps if we did spend any length of time alone we might even surprise ourselves and catch glimpses of a person who is quite a stranger to us. Listening to the feeble voice of our conscience is difficult because we are not aware that it is our conscience that disturbs us. We may feel anxious for a number of reasons, and sometimes have vague feelings of guilt, uneasiness or listlessness. Sometimes such feelings are rationalized as guilt feelings for not having done this or that, and if this guilt becomes too strong, it can find its expression in deeper anxieties which lead to mental and possibly physical illnesses such as cancer, heart disease, arthritis, etc.

One form of this anxiety concerns the fear of dying without having lived to our full potential. Another form is the fear of growing old without having truly lived; especially today when the qualities needed in a competitive world are, so we are told, youthful qualities. The fear of getting old is an expression of the feeling of living unproductively – a reaction of our conscience to the mutilation of our real selves. Another form of this anxiety is the fear of disapproval – we want to be accepted; often we want to be accepted by everybody and are afraid to deviate in thinking, feeling and acting from the cultural norms and patterns. One reason, among others, for this irrational fear of disapproval is an unconscious guilt feeling. If we cannot approve of ourselves because we fail in the task of living productively, we have to substitute approval for ourselves by trying to get the approval of others. It seems that we can cut ourselves off from hearing the voice of conscience. However, there is one state when we cannot do this and this is when we are asleep. The voice of conscience cannot be silenced and it emerges in our dreams.

Review

We are all possessors of humanistic conscience and victims of authoritarian conscience. For, example a young woman's father wants her to be a chartered accountant but she wants to make a go of working full-time with her music. She may feel consciously guilty for not having pleased the authorities (i.e. her father), while unconsciously she feels guilty for not living up to her own expectations and ambitions. However, these unconscious guilt feelings will be repressed and the patterns of our culture support this repression. According to social standards, it makes sense to feel guilty for neglecting one's self. Another reason why she might repress her guilt is the fear that by accepting it, she would be forced to take her own life seriously and free herself rather than oscillating between the fear of an angry father and attempts to satisfy herself.

If conscience is based upon a very rigid and powerful irrational authority the development of humanistic conscience can be almost entirely suppressed. A person then becomes completely dependent on external powers and ceases to feel responsible for his or her own existence. All that matters then is the approval or disapproval by these powers – which can be a state, a religion, a parent, a peer group or even friends. Even the most unethical behaviour can be justified as 'duty' in the authoritarian sense. The behaviour of Hitler's henchmen at Belsen or Auschwitz is a prime example.

Christian views of conscience

Traditionally, Christian ethics has justified moral judgements by the use of reason, and conscience has been the name given to the power of that reason brought to bear on moral issues. It is 'conscience that must always be obeyed'. However, no claim is made that conscience is infallible or will necessarily provide certainty. The teaching has traditionally been accompanied by the call for the development of an informed conscience by living in the Christian community and making use of Tradition, Scripture and Spirit in sensitizing and developing an awareness of conscience. However, some critics argue that the moral faculty (conscience) has only a limited range of operations, and on many matters we 'have no conscience'.

Moreover, it can vary considerably from person to person, and culture to culture, seeming to depend on cultural conditioning or moral training, i.e. relativism rears its head again (see pages 96–7). So what is the reliability of this moral faculty called conscience? While Joseph Butler saw conscience as a universal moral faculty, it can sometimes be weak, variable, misinformed and even defective; perhaps merely indicating a 'moral point of view' by which we struggle to make rational judgements about moral issues. However, through the ages Christians have striven and sought to find real conscience:

I do not understand my own actions. For I do not do what I want, but I do the very thing I hate … I can will what is right, but I cannot do it. For I do not do the good I want, but the evil I do not want is what I do.

St Paul in Romans 7:15–19

He who acts against his conscience sins.

St Thomas Aquinas

Since God hath assumed to himself the power and dominion of the conscience, who alone can rightly instruct and govern it, therefore it is not lawful for any whatsoever, by virtue of any authority or principality of this world, to force the consciences of others.

The Chief Principles of the Christian Religion, as Professed by the People called the Quakers, XIV (1678)

St Jerome (347–420 CE), one of the early Christian 'Fathers of the Church', spoke about the innate power capable of distinguishing good from evil as the 'spark of conscience … by which we discern that we sin'. It later became usual for Christian thinkers to use the term conscience (*conscientia*) for the ability to distinguish good from bad at the level of particular actions. St Augustine saw conscience as an innate faculty which reveals God's moral law as inscribed in the human soul, and in the thirteenth century Aquinas regarded conscience as equivalent to 'right' reason (*recta ratio*).

Augustine's account of conscience is closely related to many ancient mystical traditions, including Plato's *Republic* and the writings of Plotinus (204–69 CE) and Origen (185–255 CE), in the idea of moral purification as resulting in a 'flight of the soul' away from the world. According to Augustine, God endows each human being with a conscience whereby he or she may know the moral law. However, this knowledge by itself is insufficient. *Virtue* requires that the will should also be turned towards the good. God's grace illuminates the soul by a revelation of God's goodness, which *induces* virtue as the soul becomes charged with love for God's perfection. It is only by **grace** that the soul flies away from the world.

Although conscience was seen to reveal the moral law, medieval and Renaissance thought interpreted moral law in two different ways:

a Conscience is a form of knowledge which enables a person to examine and discern states of affairs which constitute moral facts in the same way as the scientific method examines the facts which make up biology or physics.
b Conscience is a way of coming to know and understand what God wills, rather like consulting a textbook to discover something.

John MacQuarrie, a modern theologian, distinguishes three kinds of conscience.

Firstly, conscience 'wrestling with some particular decision'; secondly, conscience as a more generalized knowledge of right and wrong (*synderesis*); and thirdly, conscience as a special and fundamental mode of self-awareness, the awareness of 'how it is with oneself'. MacQuarrie argues that the basic function of conscience is 'to disclose us to ourselves', and that as well as disclosing things it is also a call or summons. Although conscience is commonly thought of as commanding us *to do* certain things, the fundamental command of conscience is *to be – what we seek to do in any particular situation depends on what we seek to be*. Sometimes authentic conscience may come into conflict with conventional morality. For example, conventional morality accepted slavery, but William Wilberforce (1759–1833) and Abraham Lincoln (1809–65) acted according to conscience and worked for its abolition.

Review

Believers and nonbelievers approaching moral decision-making may come up with similar conclusions. However, when it comes to theorizing about *how* they arrived at a similar position, they may disagree: the believer may regard the results of this inquiry as revealing God's will – 'the voice of conscience' being understood as 'the voice of God' 'written on the heart' (Romans 2:15); whereas the nonbeliever asserts that his or her decision was dependent on his or her own reasoning alone.

Morality can be subjective or objective. **Objective morality** *is the same for all men everywhere.* **Subjective morality** *is different in different countries and at different periods. Everyone defines subjective morality differently. What one person calls 'good' is called by another 'bad', and vice versa. Subjective morality is*

also a stick with two ends; it can be turned this way and that. From the time when men appeared on the earth, from the time of Adam, there began to be formed in us with the help of God, of Nature, and our surroundings, an organ whose function is conscience. Every man has this organ, and whoever is guided by his conscience lives according to the precepts of the inner voice. But man lives according to the whim of subjective conscience, which, like subjective morality, is different everywhere. Objective conscience is not a stick with two ends, it is a realization of what is good and bad formed in us through the ages. But it happens that this organ, for many reasons, is covered by a kind of crust which can only be broken by intense suffering; then conscience speaks. But after a time man calms down, and again the organ is covered up. In ordinary circumstances a strong shock is needed for the organ to be uncovered. For example, a man's mother dies, and he begins to hear the voice of conscience. To love, honour, and cherish one's mother is the duty of every man. But man is seldom a good son. When his mother dies he remembers how he behaved towards her and he begins to suffer from remorse. Man is also a great swine, and like a swine he soon forgets; conscience sinks down again and he begins to live in his usual automatic way. He who has no conscience cannot be truly moral.

George Gurdjieff (1866–1949)

EXAM QUESTIONS

1 Is belief in God essential to morality?
[Oxford and Cambridge, 1998]

2 **a** Explain the theory of natural law.
  b Discuss the view that natural moral law is a complete guide to moral decision making. [NEAB, June 1995]

3 'Whatever God commands is good, and it is good because God commands it'. Critically examine this understanding of the relationship between religion and morality. [NEAB, June 1997]

4 Study the passage below and then answer the questions which follow.

But allowing that mankind hath the rule of right within himself, yet it may be asked, 'What obligations are we under to attend to and follow it?' I answer: it has been proved that man by his nature is a law to himself, without the particular distinct consideration of the positive sanctions of that law; the rewards and punishments which we feel, and those which from the light of reason we have ground to believe, are annexed to it. The question then carries its own answer along with it. Your obligation to obey this law, is its being the law of your nature. That your conscience approves of and attests to such a course of action, is itself alone an obligation. Conscience does not only offer itself to show us the way we should walk in,

but it likewise carries its own authority with it, that it is our natural guide; the guide assigned us by the Author of our nature; it therefore belongs to our condition of being, it is our duty to walk in that path, and follow this guide, without looking about to see whether we may not possibly forsake them with impunity.

Source: J. Butler, '*Fifteen Sermons*', Bell & Sons (1964), p. 64.

a What is meant by 'conscience'?
b Comment on the description of conscience as 'the guide assigned us by the Author of our nature'.
c Evaluate the claim that it is our duty to 'follow this guide'. [EDEXCEL, 1997]

5 Discuss the view that conscience is just the name for something which really cannot be defined. [EDEXCEL, 1997]

6 'Conscience doth make cowards of us all.' How highly should conscience be regarded as a guide to ethical behaviour? [Oxford and Cambridge, 1997]

3 Christian ethics

Despite sharing similar views about the nature of God, Christians, since the Reformation, have disagreed about a whole series of moral issues. Today is no exception and within the Christian community there is disagreement on issues around abortion, sexual ethics, artificial insemination, genetic engineering, etc.

These differences often arise out of the way Christians arrive at their values: firstly, the Christian who deplores the state of the modern world (the way in which secular values have eroded and replaced Christian values) and so holds fast to *traditional* values – what he or she might call 'eternal values', which he or she believes remain true whatever the time or place; and secondly, the Christian who *adapts* his or her approach and understanding to compromise with contemporary ways of thinking. This has been reflected in modern theology by theologians like Rudolf Bultmann (1884–1976) who argued that the task of the modern Christian is to remove the apparently mythical layers of the Bible stories (*to demythologize*), so that the essence (*the kerygma*) and heart of the Gospel message may be discovered.

THE WORD OF GOD

ALL religions have sacred scriptures. The most important source of moral principles for Christians is the Holy Bible. Nothing illustrates the conflict between the modern and traditional better than the Christian's view of the Bible. Although most Christians would agree that the Bible is in some way 'God's word' and has authority, some important issues arise. What does it mean to say the Bible is the Word of God? Is the Bible infallible (without error) because it is God's word? People who call themselves Christians interpret the Bible differently: for example, 'It is the Word of God [literalism] and has absolute authority and is to be obeyed'; or 'It has lost some of its meaning in translation so needs to be interpreted, not just for the words themselves, but in the light of our modern thinking'; or 'It is a historical document reflecting values that were relevant when it was written but irrelevant today'. Although Christians might disagree about interpretation, there are some basic principles that they agree on in both the Old and New Testaments.

- The world has purpose and meaning: 'In the beginning God created the Heavens and the Earth' (Genesis Chapter 1).
- Morality is an objective reality which is intrinsically part of the nature of things. God made humans in 'His image'. We are responsible moral agents ultimately answerable to God.
- We have been endowed with conscience (see pages 30–2) – 'the voice of God within' – which provides us with an intuitive awareness of right and wrong. However, according to Genesis Chapter 3 this harmony is shattered by 'The Fall' which led to disharmony, disruption, death, disintegration, chaos, conflict, the burial of conscience and ignorance of Natural Law. This terrible state is overcome only when God enters into a binding relationship with his people – The Covenant – promising to help restore harmony on the condition that people live according to His commandments.
- God reveals his standards by means of rules for living which are found in the Pentateuch (The Books of Genesis, Exodus, Leviticus, Numbers and Deuteronomy). They are encapsulated by the Ten Commandments:

1 I am the Lord your God.
2 You shall have no other gods before me.
3 You shall not make for yourself a
   graven image.
4 You shall not take the name of the Lord

in vain. Observe the sabbath day, to
keep it holy.
5 Honour your father and your mother.
6 You shall not kill.
7 Neither shall you commit adultery.
8 Neither shall you steal.
9 Neither shall you bear false witness
   against your neighbour.
10 Neither shall you covet.

(Exodus 20:1–17)

Profound ethical teachings can also be found in the Books of Proverbs, Job, Ecclesiastes and the Song of Solomon (known as Wisdom Literature); and in the utterings of the Prophets (Hosea, Micah, Amos, Isaiah, Jeremiah) who taught that religion and justice, equality and compassion are all one and the same.

- At the heart of New Testament ethics is the theme of Redemption. God, revealing himself in and through creation, in the law and through his prophets, now fully reveals himself in human form as Jesus Christ who lives and dies for the redemption of humankind. The life and teachings of Jesus become the essence of Christian morality. Christians who want to discover how best to live only need to look to the example of Jesus who, according to tradition, is God incarnate. As well as being a moral exemplar Jesus is also the Messiah ushering in a *new* **Kingdom of God**. He is portrayed as being the living exemplar of Kingdom Ethics, his miracles and teachings recorded signs of the Kingdom. Jesus is depicted as proclaiming 'Light' and 'New Life' in contrast to darkness and death; teaching a community ethic built on love, forgiveness and loyalty: 'Love one another, as I have loved you' (John 15:12), the essence of the life of the Kingdom being love or *agape* (self-giving concern for others).

Some of the most challenging of Jesus' teachings are to be found in the Sermon on the Mount (Matthew Chapters 5–7), which focus on ethical conduct in our daily life and how it affects our destiny in the next life.

Chapter 5 begins with *The Beatitudes* which emphasize the spirit in which the children of the Kingdom should live, for example 'Blessed are those who hunger and thirst for righteousness, for they shall be satisfied' (5:6); 'Blessed are the peacemakers, for they shall be called Sons of God' (5:9).

Jesus teaches that it is not just the outer rules and laws that must be obeyed but the inner spirit of the law: Jesus' teachings are more than a set of commandments, but a challenge to the inner world of deeper motivation and intent. It is not how people act that is all-important – *inner intention and attitude are crucial too.*

In Chapter 6 Jesus explains to the Children of the Kingdom how they should fulfil laws and customs: 'When you give alms, do not let your left hand know what your right hand is doing, so that your alms may be in secret' (6:3). In the same chapter he calls for detachment from the material and sensual world of wealth, ambition and power: 'Do not lay up for yourselves treasures on earth, where moth and rust consume and where thieves break in and steal, but lay up for yourselves treasure in heaven ... For where your treasure is, there will your heart be also' (6:19–21), a teaching that is in stark contrast to modern capitalism, where profit is deemed more important than principle.

The Golden Rule (see page 97) appears in Chapter 7 alongside such teachings as: 'Why do you see the speck in your brother's eye, but do not notice the log that is in your own eye?' (7:3); and teachings on the Kingdom: 'Enter by the narrow gate; for the gate is wide and the way is easy that leads to destruction, and those who enter by it are many. For the gate is narrow and the way is hard, that leads to life, and those who find it are few' (7:14).

The Sermon on the Mount has inspired generations of Christians and non-Christians alike. It expresses a demanding ethic requiring deep sincerity rather than the assumption that 'because someone follows the rules he or she is necessarily a good person'. In contrast to much contemporary secular thought the Sermon puts enormous emphasis on the inner man or woman – the intention which proceeds from the heart rather than the outward act itself. The psychology of the individual becomes all-important – what motivates people deep down is crucial and not just what appears on the surface of 'personality'. These inner attitudes and motives have a direct bearing on the way people act in the external world, and are at the heart of Jesus' ethical teaching.

St Ambrose (340–96 CE), an early Christian theologian, explained this divine responsibility in *The Duties of the Clergy*:

When a Christian meets with an armed robber he cannot return his blows, lest in defending his life he should stain his love toward his neighbour. The verdict on this is plain and clear in the books of the Gospel ... What robber is more hateful than the persecutor who came to kill Christ? But Christ would not be defended by the wounds of the persecutor, for He willed to heal all by His wounds.

The Fourth Gospel

The Gospel According to St John was composed about 90 CE. It is sometimes called the 'spiritual Gospel', and according to Johannine tradition contains the secret teaching received orally by John from Christ. It celebrates Christ as the *Logos* or Word of God as well as the 'Wisdom' of God, grounding Jesus in his earthly historical context:

In the beginning was the Word: the Word was with God and the Word was God.

John 1:1

The use of the 'Logos' (*The Word*) suggests a dynamic principle by which all things come through Him. *The Word* itself is light entering the world, empowering people to become children of God. John is clearly describing 'a new' creation story, one which echoes the creation story in Genesis in its opening words, 'In the beginning'. *The Word* is with God 'In the beginning' just as wisdom and truth is. The Fourth Gospel does not express a rule-centred ethic but is concerned with the revelation of the nature of God through Jesus Christ. The moral imperative of the Gospel is to 'Believe the truth and do the truth'; and it presents stark contrasts: light versus darkness; freedom versus slavery; courage versus fear; implying that he or she who possesses spiritual insight *does the truth*:

> *This is my commandment, that you love*
> *one another as I have loved you.*
> *Greater love than this hath no man, than*
> *that a man bestow his life for his friends.*
> *You are my friends, if you do whatsoever I*
> *command you.*

> John 15:12–14

Fig. 3.1 'This is my commandment, that you love one another as I have loved you'

St Paul's teaching

Paul does not present his ethical principles in a systematic way, but stresses the relationship between ethics and theology. For St Paul moral behaviour is linked with belief in judgement and resurrection, whereby decisions are made, with a profound awareness of death. The kernel of Paul's moral advice is *faith working itself out in love*; expressed in the beautiful passage on *agape* in I Corinthians 13:1–3.

> *If I speak in the tongues of men and of*
> *angels, but have not love, I am a noisy gong*
> *or a clanging cymbal. And if I have*
> *prophetic powers, and understand all*
> *mysteries and all knowledge, and if I have*
> *all faith, so as to remove mountains, but*
> *have not love, I am nothing. If I give away*
> *all I have and if I deliver my body to be*
> *burned, but have not love, I gain nothing.*

St Paul teaches that love fulfils God's law: 'love does no wrong to a neighbour; therefore love is the fulfilling of the law' (Romans 13:10); his ethic is a community ethic – Christians becoming the 'body' of Christ, God's 'field', 'vineyard' and 'temple' which is also representative of physical existence, with the body itself being 'the temple of the holy spirit', something to be honoured and cared for. In 1 Corinthians 15 he expresses the view that resurrection is the key to the defeat of death, and this life is a process to be completed, 'a gymnasium' in which even suffering is transformed: '... and we also rejoice in our sufferings, because we know that suffering produces endurance, and endurance produces character' (Romans 5:3); and in the end *all will be well* as 'God works for good with those who love him' (Romans 8:28).

How does the Bible contribute to ethics?

- It gives Christians a theological basis for moral obligations, in terms of the individual's obligations to do the will of God.
- It provides Christians with an account of the relation of morality to God's purposes in creation, explaining how God's purpose is hindered by wrong living and how God's grace can restore righteous living.
- It depicts the ideals of the Kingdom of God that Christ came to establish.
- It reveals God's moral law, declaring duties in many aspects of life.
- It teaches principles of human justice, love and mercy, reflecting God's nature.

TRADITION AS A SOURCE OF MORAL TEACHING ■

'THE Church' literally means an assembly of people, a believing community, which carries on the work of Jesus Christ in response to his teaching. Although the Church exists in the world, it should ideally not be 'of the world' but a living example of the presence and power of the Kingdom of God. Sadly, this has not always been the case (see page 23). Over the centuries, after divisions and disagreements on doctrinal matters, the Christian Church developed three main traditions:

- the Roman Catholic Church
- the Orthodox Church
- the Protestant or Reformed Churches.

These three 'families' of Christianity placed different emphasis on tradition as a source of guidance on moral issues. Protestant Churches stress the importance of the Bible as the most important source of moral teaching, whereas Orthodox and Catholic Christians believe that God's teachings have been safeguarded by the Church both in terms of its interpretation of scripture and in its historical practices. The appeal of looking to tradition as a source of guidance is not just because of the tradition itself, but also because of the reality and relevance of the authority behind the tradition.

Roman Catholic Christians believe that the Pope has special authority and that he is *infallible* (without error) when he speaks to, and in the name of, the Church on questions of faith or ethics. Tradition therefore reflects the historical experiences of the Church. It attempts to interpret ethics as expressions of understanding about God and Jesus Christ and depends on a God-given rationality which enables men and women to make reasoned generalizations from one situation to another. It provides Christians with a firm base for moral teaching and the wisdom and knowledge of thinkers and theologians throughout the ages.

The Ecumenical Movement aims to bring different traditions together by reminding Christians that at the heart of Christian ethics lie the following principles:

- The Christian Life is a response in the Holy Spirit to God's self-giving in Jesus Christ. We are made in the image of God.
- God creates human beings with the dignity of persons in community, and calls them to a life of responsibility and freedom, endowing them with the hope of happiness. As children of God, true freedom is to be found in service.
- Ignorance and sin have led to the misuse and corruption of human freedom.
- The true goal of the moral life is the flourishing and fulfilment of that humanity for which all men and women have been created. The fundamental moral question, therefore, is, not 'What ought we to do?', but *'What kind of moral persons are we called to become?'*. For Christians moral obedience is nourished by the hope of becoming like God.
- True **personhood** has its origins and roots in the life and love of God.

THE HOLY SPIRIT AS A SOURCE OF MORALITY ■

CHRISTIANS believe that the Spirit is the life-giving breath of God whereby the lower communicates with the higher and the higher with the lower. It is an energy and a life-giving force that reveals God's creative work in the world. The New Testament view of ethics is closely related to the belief that the Higher, God's Holy Spirit, guides, teaches and leads the believer into truth: '... the Counsellor, the Holy Spirit, whom the Father will send in my name, he will teach you all things' (John 14:26). In the early chapters of Acts in the New Testament the giving of the Spirit at

Pentecost is described, fulfilling the Old Testament prophecy of Jeremiah: 'I will put my law within them, and I will write it upon their hearts' (Jeremiah 31:33).

For the early Christians the power of the Spirit strengthened their resolve to pursue their beliefs and inspired their inner moral guide. However, the Bible makes no direct reference to nuclear weapons, multinational corporations, genetic engineering, mass advertising, the Internet, satellite TV, chemical and biological weapons, industrial pollution, space missions, in vitro fertilization (IVF), surrogacy or **cloning**. How then can modern Christians find guidance on these issues? If there is no tradition within the Church to draw on, how might they look to the work of the Holy Spirit for moral guidance? This approach of responding to 'the workings of the spirit' is not without its dangers – it could be reduced to a purely subjective response coloured by personal preference. For example, one scientist who is a Christian might feel that the Spirit moves him to accept genetic engineering, whereas another might argue that the same Spirit has moved her to condemn it. The Church, therefore, has to ensure that it can provide a framework within which such views can be discussed.

JESUS CHRIST

F OR all Christians the person of Jesus represents the supreme moral exemplar, the perfect man, the noble man. Jesus is both God incarnate and a man who understands our deepest fears and weaknesses – a relationship profoundly expressed by Blaise Pascal, the French philosopher and mathematician, in *Pensées*:

The Christian religion ... teaches men these truths; that there is a God whom men can know, and that there is a corruption in their nature which renders them unworthy of Him. It is equally important to men to know

both these points; and it is equally dangerous for man to know God without knowing his own wretchedness, and to know his own wretchedness without knowing the Redeemer who can free him from it. The knowledge of only one of these points gives rise to the pride of philosophers, who have known God, and not their own wretchedness, or to the despair of atheists, who know their own wretchedness, but not the Redeemer ... We can have an excellent knowledge of God without that of wretchedness and of our own wretchedness without that of God. But we cannot know Jesus Christ without knowing at the same time both God and our own wretchedness.

For discussion

There are sometimes glaring differences in the essential moral content of Christianity and in the values espoused by modern society. The dilemma facing the modern Christian is: can he or she be both modern and Christian? This raises issues about the content of Christian morality. But where do Christian moral principles come from? How might a Christian use the principles of Christian ethics to form a judgement on issues raised?

CRITICISMS OF CHRISTIAN ETHICS

'Christian ethics breed intolerance'

Historically, there is much evidence to support this criticism, as different churches have at times persecuted each other as well as people of other faiths. The activities of some missionaries, too, has left much to be desired, especially in their arrogant assumption that only Christian teachings can lead to the 'Good'. Ludwig Feuerbach, the nineteenth-century thinker, wrote:

Wherever morality is based on theology, wherever the right is made dependent on divine authority, the most immoral, unjust, infamous things can be justified and established.

'Christian ethics are built on fear, and a system of reward or punishment'

Traditionally, churches have taught that immoral behaviour is punished in the torments of 'hell and damnation', frightening people to conform out of fear and not allowing them the liberty to strive for inner conviction:

So in saying that things are not good by any rule of goodness, but sheerly by the grace of God, it seems to me that one destroys, without realising it, all the love of God and his glory. For why praise him for what he has done if he would be equally praiseworthy in doing exactly the contrary.

Leibniz, *Discourse on Metaphysics* (1686)

'Christian ethics are repressive'

Sometimes Christian ethics are viewed as a set of 'do nots', interpreted in a life-denying way, making them appear restrictive and curtailing individual autonomy and freedom. Bertrand Russell described the effects of repressive ethics thus: 'We are heirs to the conscience – vivisection and self-crucifixion of two thousand years'.

'Christian ethics make people weak'

Christian ethics make people weak, leading them to stock moral reactions and preventing them from learning from their own experiences and mistakes. The Prussian philosopher Friedrich Nietzsche despised Christian values. Christianity, Nietzsche argued, had led to a systematic devaluation of this world in favour of the next, and thus to a false spirituality. Nietzsche declared that 'God is dead' – a stark recognition that people only

worship subjective morality. Christians exalt the virtues of the weak, the humble, the poor, the oppressed, not because they love these people but because of their own psychological dysfunctions – their hidden hatred of strength, their fear of life, and their complacency, vanity and pride:

Your neighbour-love is your bad love of yourselves. Ye flee unto your neighbour from yourselves and would fain make a virtue thereof! But I fathom your 'unselfishness' ... You cannot stand yourselves, and you do not love yourselves sufficiently.

F. Nietzsche, *Beyond Good and Evil*

But 'God is dead', says Nietzsche, and thus the sanction of traditional slave morality is gone.

All the modern ethical theories (see pages 42–57) are forms of self-deception, according to Nietzsche. Kantian ethics, for example, attempts to give the endorsement of universal law to the individualist's moral attitudes: 'Kant wanted to prove in a way that would dumbfound the "common man" that the "common man" was right.' But Nietzsche's accusation is that in fact Kant assumes what he sets out to prove. He takes it for granted that we are entitled to make moral judgements and inquires what must be the case if that is so; Kant never asks, as Nietzsche does, whether we are so *entitled*. *Who* do we think we are to make moral judgements? In trying to bind others by universal moral judgements, we pretend to be speaking in the name of purely practical reason, but we are in fact using these judgements to justify our own weakness.

The utilitarians are also attacked: 'Man does not seek happiness; only the Englishman does that.' Power not happiness is the fundamental human goal according to Nietzsche. Sympathetic interpreters of the Nietzschean 'will to power' have insisted that by power Nietzsche does not mean power over others; he saw the ideal expression of power in the type of personality which has the limitations of self-love, yet by an act of will is still able to affirm itself. It is when the will to power is not allowed expression, but is hidden and repressed, that it turns into a drive against others, summoning up ideals in the name of which such oppression can be carried out. The type of personality who has conquered self-love, yet remains in essence unconquerable, is a Superman (*Ubermensch*): 'The Superman is the meaning of the earth. Let your will say: The Superman shall be the meaning of the earth!' From this moment, according to Nietzsche, we can not only *choose* our own values but also become the *creators* of values.

EXAM QUESTIONS

1 Is the Bible the only reliable foundation for morality?   [Oxford and Cambridge, 1996]

2 How may Christians' claim to guidance by the Holy Spirit be verified?
[EDEXCEL, 1996]

3 **a** What are the grounds for holding the view that there is a fundamental unity between religion and morality.
   b State and evaluate the argument put forward against this view.
[EDEXCEL, 1995]

4 Can our actions be good, unless our motives are pure?   [EDEXCEL, 1996]

5 'If God exists, there might be special and acceptable reasons for being moral.'
   a Examine why belief in God provides reasons for being moral.
   b Explain and evaluate the difficulties raised by these reasons.
(EDEXCEL,1996)

6 'Religious Principles do not guide believers to the right decision. Rather they allow believers to justify almost any action in the name of their faith.' Discuss this statement, illustrating your answer with reference to two moral issues.
[NEAB, 1997]

decision followed by a truly ethical action would be one which produced the greatest pleasure. According to Bentham, pleasure and pain are measured by the hedonic or utility calculus whereby the following criteria are taken into account:

- How long does it last? – DURATION.
- How intense is it? – INTENSITY
- How near is it? – REMOTENESS
- How sure are we that it will come? – CERTAINTY
- How free from pain is it? – PURITY
- How much will it lead to more pleasure? – RICHNESS
- How widely does it cover? – EXTENT

Bentham argued that it is possible, therefore, to give specific content to ideas about right and wrong by reference to the *amount* of pleasure and pain that is involved in particular situations. **Classical utilitarianism** – the theory defended by both Bentham and Mill – can be summarized in three propositions:

a Actions are to be judged right or wrong solely by virtue of their consequences. Nothing else matters. Right actions are simply those that have the best consequences.

b In assessing consequences the only thing that matters is the amount of happiness or unhappiness that is caused. Everything else is irrelevant. Thus right actions are those that produce the greatest balance of happiness over unhappiness.

c In calculating happiness or unhappiness, no one's happiness is to be counted as more important than anyone else's. Each person's welfare is equally important.

Thus, right actions are those that produce the greatest possible balance of happiness over unhappiness, with each person's happiness counted as equally important. Utilitarianism has been a hugely popular theory, and continues to be widely accepted and applied today, even though it has been challenged by a number of arguments.

'Anti-utilitarian' arguments are so convincing that some philosophers have concluded that utilitarianism must be abandoned. However, despite the arguments, many thinkers refuse to let the theory go. According to modern utilitarians, the anti-utilitarian arguments show that the classical theory needs only to be *modified*, remoulded and recast into a more satisfactory form as the basic concept of utilitarianism is correct and should therefore be preserved.

Is 'happiness' all that matters?

The question 'What things are good?' is not necessarily the same as the question 'What actions are right?'. Utilitarianism answers the second question by referring back to the first one. Right actions, it says, are the ones that produce the most good. Again that old question arises: 'What is good?' The classical utilitarian reply according to Mill is: 'The utilitarian doctrine is that happiness is desirable, and the only thing desirable, as an end; all other things being desirable as means to that end.'

The idea that happiness is the ultimate good (and unhappiness the ultimate evil) is known as **hedonism**. Hedonism has always been an attractive theory because it expresses the idea that things are good or bad only on account of the way they make us feel. However, there are serious flaws to hedonism. Hedonism misunderstands the nature of happiness. Happiness is not something that is always *recognized* as good and sought for its own sake, with other factors appreciated only as a means of bringing happiness about. Instead, happiness is a *response* we have. This is very different from first setting out after happiness, then deciding what to do to make us happy, and then deliberately doing it, making it merely a means to an end.

Happiness is the ultimate good (Hedonism)

I maintain that if the discoveries of Kepler and Newton could not have been made known except by sacrificing the lives of one, a dozen, a hundred or more men, Newton would have had the right, would indeed have been duty bound ... to eliminate the dozen or the hundred for the sake of making his discoveries known to the whole of humanity ... But if such a one is forced for the sake of his idea to step over a corpse or wade through blood, he can, I maintain, find within himself, in his conscience, a sanction for wading through blood. That depends on the idea and its dimensions, of course.

Raskalnikov in Fyodor Dostoyevsky's
Crime and Punishment (1866)

Today there are few contemporary philosophers who would call themselves Hedonists. Those sympathetic to utilitarianism have tried to formulate their view without adopting a hedonistic account of good and evil. The English philosopher, G. E. Moore (see pages 5–6), tried to compile a short list of things to be regarded as good in themselves, i.e. intrinsic goods: pleasure, friendship and aesthetic enjoyment – and that right actions are those that create such things.

Other utilitarians have tried to bypass the question of how many things are good in themselves, leaving it an open question. They argue that right actions are the ones that have the best results, however we measure goodness. This view is sometimes called ideal utilitarianism, which accepts general principles and rules (for example 'You shall not kill'), arguing that these principles have themselves been framed on utilitarian grounds. Still others try to bypass the question in another way, arguing that we should act so as to maximize the satisfaction of people's *preferences* (this is called preference utilitarianism). The preferences of the person concerned in each case should be taken into account, thus allowing people to say what for them constitutes pleasure or pain.

Criticisms of utilitarianism

Utilitarianism claims that only consequences matter. The most fundamental idea underlying the theory is that in order to determine whether an action is right, *we should look at what will happen as a result of doing it.* If it were to turn out that some *other* matter is also important in determining rightness, then utilitarianism would be undermined at its very foundation. The most serious anti-utilitarian arguments attack the theory at just this point, arguing that various other considerations, in addition to utility, are important in determining whether actions are right:

a *Justice.* Utilitarianism can sometimes be incompatible with the ideal of justice. Justice requires that we treat people fairly, according to their individual needs and merits. The classic illustration of how utilitarianism can appear wrong to those who hold *justice as fairness* has been given in this form:

    ... let us imagine that the happiness of the whole human race were to be immeasurably increased – poverty eliminated, brotherhood achieved, disease

version of the theory, which gives rules a greater importance than they merit. Act-utilitarianism is, however, recognized to be a radical doctrine which implies that many of our ordinary moral feelings may be mistaken. In this respect, it does what good philosophy always does – it challenges us to rethink matters that we have previously taken for granted.

There is sense in which no moral philosopher can completely reject utilitarianism, for the consequences of our actions – whether they promote happiness, or cause misery – are obviously extremely important. John Stuart Mill once remarked that, insofar as we are benevolent, we must accept the utilitarian standard. Moreover, the utilitarian emphasis on impartiality must also be a part of any defensible moral theory. The question is whether these are the *only* kinds of considerations an adequate theory must acknowledge. Are there not other considerations that are also important?

If we look at what Smart calls our 'common moral consciousness' (see page 53) it seems that there are *many* other considerations that are morally important. But the radical act-utilitarians are right to warn us that 'common sense' cannot always be trusted.

The strength of utilitarianism is that by sticking to the Principle of Utility as the *only* standard for judging right and wrong, it avoids incorporating into ethical theory prejudices, feelings, and foggy 'intuitions' that may have no rational basis. However, despite the many social, political and economic advances brought about by utilitarianism, the utility calculus is not always a reliable tool for moral understanding, as people do not function in this clinical way when faced with life-changing choices.

For discussion

People in Britain, the USA and elsewhere once believed that slavery made 'common sense', and they might even have insisted that an adequate moral theory should

---

accommodate this 'fact'. In modern times no one worth listening to would hold such views. But who knows how many other irrational prejudices are still a part of our 'moral common sense':

There must be still other countless errors of the same sort that no living man can yet detect, because of the fog within which our type of Western culture envelops us. Cultural influences have set up the assumptions about the mind, the body, and the universe with which we begin; pose the questions we ask; influence the facts we seek; determine the interpretation we give these facts; and direct our reaction to these interpretations and conclusions.

Gunnar Myrdal, *An American Dilemma* (1941)

Christian responses to utilitarianism

- Mill believed that his utilitarian ethic had caught the very spirit of the Golden Rule (to treat others as we would want them to treat us) (see pages 97–8). However, Christian love knows no limit and is prepared to go not one mile but two. To love one's neighbour as if he or she were oneself, to put oneself in his or her place, is certainly not to treat him or her as one of many. Utilitarians define 'justice' as treating 'similar cases similarly' whereas Christian ethics means 'treating similar cases dissimilarly', regarding the good of any individual as *more* than their own.
- Christian ethics differs from utilitarianism in the importance each gives to the problem '*Whose* good'? While utilitarians answer this question with '*What* is the good?', Christian ethics answers it with '*Whose*?'. For utilitarians love is subordinate to justice, whereas for Christians love is primary.
- A fundamental difference between utilitarianism and Christian ethics can be seen in the events around the trial of Jesus before Caiaphas, as recorded in

John's Gospel (Chapter 18). Jesus and Caiaphas act from totally different ethical principles, even though they might have spoken the same words: 'It is expedient that one man should die for the people' (John 18:14). But Caiaphas applied this principle to the other person, whereas Jesus applied it to himself. Caiaphas was concerned to maintain an existing social order, whereas Jesus was concerned to bring reconciliation and community where before there had been none.

- While utilitarianism aims to preserve and create an ordered and just social order, this is not always sufficient for bringing in an isolated or hostile individual into that community. Christians believe that only love can penetrate the barriers that often exist between people. It is *relationship* that is ultimately important, and only by loving another for their own sake can true community come into being.

Universal ethical egoism

Ethical egoism argues that everyone ought to act in his or her own self-interest. *My act is right if it is in my self-interest and wrong if it is not in my self-interest. Your act is right if it is in your self-interest and wrong if it is not.* This version of the theory is called universal ethical egoism since it is supposed to apply to everyone equally.

Another possible version of universal ethical egoism is personal ethical egoism, where I say that *I ought to do those actions that most benefit me*, but I have nothing to say about your actions. This is not really an ethical theory, but more like a personal philosophy of life. Still another version is individual ethical egoism, where I say that you and I both ought to do what is in my self-interest. This view involves a strange asymmetry: *you ought always to help me, but I should never help you, unless that benefits me.*

Can egoism provide an ethic by which society can live harmoniously or would it lead to anarchy? Can the ethical egoist be trusted to do what is good for others?

The standard criticism of universal ethical egoism is that it involves a contradiction, although this alleged contradiction is not always easy to spot. Suppose Terry and Mary are arguing. As a practising universal ethical egoist, I tell Terry to win (since that is in his self-interest), but I also then tell Mary that she should win (since that is in her self-interest). But they *both* cannot win, so there is something odd about this advice. Nevertheless, it is not formally self-contradictory to tell them both to try to win.

None of these views should be confused with **psychological egoism**, which holds that everyone will ultimately do what is in their self-interest, which is actually not an ethical theory but a description and claim about *how* people act. Psychological egoism seizes on the fact that people are generally motivated by self-interest. The ethical egoist argues that because people are motivated by self-interest then they ought to pursue their own good as deliberately and effectively as they can. Note the step in this argument from a psychological generalization taken as 'fact' – i.e. 'people are motivated by self-interest' – to ethical 'ought', from a description to a prescriptive obligation. This is a doubtful logical inference. However, ethical egoists would defend this move as being a recognition of the psychological condition of humanity. But is this true? Are we all driven ultimately by self-interest?

If it is put forward as a universally valid description then it only needs one counter-example to deny it. Many Christians would argue that history is ennobled by such people – Jesus Christ, the saints and martyrs. The egoist may counter this by saying that unselfish acts may still be in one's own interest and may provide a great deal of satisfaction or ego-fulfilment. But again Christians would argue that this is a cynical view which neglects the different accounts of Jesus' life which consistently depict a Christ who *emptied* himself of self-love.

Bishop Joseph Butler (1692–1752) argued that while people do indeed desire their own inner happiness in general, motivation is tied in specific cases to particular external objects (*Fifteen Sermons upon Human Nature*, 1726). For example, 'I do not want food for the sake of my own happiness, but because I am hungry and need it to go on working, to go on serving others. Therefore, my desire for food is not self-contained and solely egotistical.' This is the difference, according to Butler, between 'true self-love' and 'unnatural or debauched self-love'. True self-love does not conflict with loving people or things for their own sake: friendship, marriage and parenthood help us develop non-egotistical motivations to such an extent that people often sacrifice their own interests for those they love. We desire their well-being as much and sometimes more than our own. The Bible teaches: 'love our neighbour as ourselves' (Luke 10:27) (and 'a husband is to love his wife as his own body' – Ephesians 5:28). Self-love therefore does not necessarily conflict with **benevolence**.

Some thinkers have argued that such a view is over-optimistic. The English political philosopher Thomas Hobbes, in his book *Leviathan*, argued that our psychological egoism has led to 'the war of all against all' and that human life in this condition is 'nasty, short and brutish'. However, it must also be recognized that despite greed, self-interest and apathy, many people have not turned their backs on helping others. Self-interest is not the whole story. What about people who dedicate their lives in service to others? Hobbes' pessimism that egoism left to itself would lead to chaos led him to argue that if society was not going to be brutal and nasty it needed enlightened self-interested benevolent monarchs in charge. But surely such rulers, like their subjects, are ultimately polluted by egoism? In his *Republic* Plato (see pages 20–1) proposed to train a ruling class in whom egoism could not take hold. Their education and socialization would all be so arranged, their economic and sexual needs so fully supplied, that self-interest would not distract their minds from justice and truth.

A Christian view of egoism

- While a legitimate psychological self-interest is assumed in the Bible, this is balanced by ethical concern for others: '*Love thy neighbour as thyself*'.
- Egoism views people much more individualistically than does Biblical teaching. We are all members of the whole, related by a common humanity, and live in *relationship* to others and to God.
- The individual egoist says we should only seek our own individual good, whereas the universal egoist says that *every* individual should always seek his or her own good. However, if individual egoists seek only their own self-interest, they could never be trusted to give advice or be elected to public office.
- The doctrine of human depravity must be balanced by the doctrine of Common Grace, i.e. God in his goodness restrains the evil possibilities inherent in a degenerative egoism, maintaining a degree of order in nature and society.
- The highest end for the Christian is not egoistic, but 'to seek first the Kingdom of God'. The highest motivation is love for God and love for neighbour.
- In *On the Trinity*, St Augustine explores the deepest implications of the Christian view of true self-love:

He therefore who loves men, ought to love them either because they are righteous, or that they may become righteous. For so also he ought to love himself, either because he is righteous, or that he may become righteous; for in this way he loves his neighbour as himself without any risk.

Review

The fundamental difference between deontological and teleological theories can be better understood by looking at Natural Law theory (a deontological theory) and Utilitarianism (a teleological theory).

The Natural Law theory (see pages 26–7) begins with theories about the nature and purpose of the world and moves on to ask about the purpose of every action or object. The right thing to do, is that which fulfils the natural purpose. Therefore, it starts from principles and applies them to situations.

Utilitarianism (see pages 49–55), on the other hand, argues that an action should be judged according to the results it achieves. It begins with the pain or pleasure involved in individual situations and then takes into account the wider pain or pleasure involved by the application of general rules, or the preferences of the people involved.

EXAM QUESTIONS

1 On what grounds might a Utilitarian seek to defend the principle of Utility?
[EDEXCEL, 1997]

2 a According to Utilitarianism what makes an action right or wrong?
b Discuss the objections a religious believer might have to this method of moral decision-making.
[NEAB, 1995]

3 How satisfactory is categorical imperativism as a theory of ethics?
[EDEXCEL, 1998]

4 Compare the ethics of Kant with the ethical teaching of Jesus.
[Oxford and Cambridge,1997]

5 a What are the distinguishing features of a deontological ethical theory?
b Compare and contrast this theory with situation ethics.   [EDEXCEL, 1996]

6 a What are the distinctive features of Situation Ethics?
b Assess the view that 'Situation Ethics provides religious believers with an adequate guide to moral decision making'.   [NEAB, 1997]

– *Jesus Christ*: any understanding of technology and ethics must focus on the person and ministry of Jesus Christ who taught the worth and dignity of human life.

For discussion

And the Lord God commanded the man, saying, 'You may freely eat of every tree of the garden; but of the tree of the knowledge of good and evil you shall not eat, for in the day that you eat of it you shall die'.

Genesis 2:16, 17

Science and technology by themselves cannot disclose the meaning of human existence and human progress ... Science and technology by their very nature require unconditional respect for fundamental moral criteria. They must be at the service of the person, of his inalienable rights, of his true and integral good, in conformity with the plan and the will of God.

Catechism of the Catholic Church (1994)

ANIMAL RIGHTS

IN 1997, according to Home Office figures, 2,635,969 animal experiments were carried out in Britain for cancer research, disease prevention and biological research, and 2,000 to test household products. Medical advances which have depended on animal research include anaesthetics, open-heart surgery, whooping cough and polio vaccines, multiple sclerosis, kidney transplants, high blood pressure drugs, psychiatric drugs, life support systems for premature babies and gene therapy.

However, the British Union for the Abolition of Vivisection (BUAV) argues that experiments are unreliable because they tell us about animals, not people, and the results produced are crude.

For discussion

QUESTION: Is it right to use animals in medical research?

Yes. Animal research in the UK is regulated by strict legislation. The animals are treated carefully and suffering is minimised. Without this work new treatments would never be tested to see if they are safe.
No. Animal experiments are wrong. You do not know if an animal is suffering. Research should be carried out without experimentation on animals, even if that slows progress.

Since the 1970s animal rights activists have argued that animals have rights and should never be used for experiments regardless of the possible benefits to humans (Fig. 5.1). They argue that simply because chimpanzees, laboratory rats and farm animals are not members of our species, that does not give us the right to abuse them and kill them for our own ends. Animal experiments can only be justified when they attempt to enhance human welfare. When their likely outcome is the shattering of life, it is a terrible waste.

Animal rights activists argue that many members of the scientific community are guilty of **speceism**: a prejudice in favour of one's own species and against other species. They ask: 'if possessing a higher

Fig. 5.1 Anti-vivisectionists argue that animals have rights

intelligence does not entitle one human to use another for his own ends, how can it entitle humans to exploit nonhumans for the same purpose?' (Peter Singer, 1975).

They also argue that there are alternatives to medical research using animals, including computer modelling, testing human cell/ tissue cultures, test tube techniques and studies of patients; and that alternative and holistic methods must be promoted, including homoeopathy, acupuncture, herbalism and chiropractic.

Just because we think of ourselves as rational, self-conscious beings, this does not give us the right to disregard the intelligence and sophisticated social awareness of the other animals we use in our experiments (Fig. 5.2). Although they may not be able to do higher mathematics, chimpanzees have the same rich emotional and social life as humans and, as they basically have the same nervous system and lower brain (the seat of emotions), are capable of feeling pain and distress in exactly the same way as us.

Theologians and philosophers have long been concerned with animal rights and nearly 800 years ago Thomas Aquinas wrote:

Hereby is refuted the error of those who said it is sinful for a man to kill dumb animals: for by divine providence they are intended for man's use in the natural order. Hence it is no wrong for man to make use of them, either by killing, or in any other way whatever ... And if any passages of Holy Writ seem to forbid us to be cruel to dumb animals, for instance to kill a bird with its young: this is either to remove men's thoughts from being cruel to other men, and lest through being cruel to animals one becomes cruel to human beings: or because injury to an animal leads to the temporal hurt of man, either of the doer of the deed, or of another: or on account of some (religious) signification: thus the Apostle expounds the prohibition against muzzling the ox that treadeth the corn.

Fig. 5.2 'We are trustees and cannot escape the obligation to act responsibly'

Six hundred years later Jeremy Bentham, social reformer and founder of utilitarianism (see pages 49–55), wrote:

The day may come when the rest of the animal creation may acquire those rights which never could have been witholden from them but by the hand of tyranny. The French have already discovered that the blackness of the skin is no reason why a human being should be abandoned without redress to the caprice of a tormentor. It may one day come to be recognized that the number of the legs, the villosity of the skin, or the termination of the os sacrum are reasons equally insufficient for abandoning a sensitive being to the same fate. What else is it that should trace the insuperable line? Is it the faculty of reason, or perhaps the faculty of discourse? But a full-grown horse or dog is beyond comparison a more donors have been screened and no record of their identity. On the Internet a website appeared in 1998 offering to match up a sperm donor selected according to individual specifications, right down to educational qualifications and income.

For discussion

Science can do many things but it can tell us nothing about what it means to be human, hence it has nothing to contribute to the great moral issues of right and wrong, or the meaning of life, which are the province of philosophy and religion.

James Le Fanu, doctor and journalist

Cloning

Controversy erupted in December 1998 when a joint report by the Human Genetics Advisory Committee and the HFEA left the door open for cloning human material for therapeutic purposes. They recommended that human reproductive cloning (i.e. permitting a fully formed human clone to be born) (Fig. 5.5) should be forbidden, but that cloning as a means of obtaining replacement tissues and organs should be permitted (i.e. for regeneration).

Ethicists want to anticipate what will be possible in ten years' time, so that the debate will be ahead of the technology. For example, will it be acceptable to allow scientists to clone an embryo of eight days old? (This would be done by removing a cell from the skin of a human and fusing its nucleus into a human egg from which the nucleus has been removed. The embryo would develop in a test tube to the point where a line of the stem cells – the basic cells which have the potential to become any part of the human body – have developed.)

The greatest advantage of cloning is that cloned material will not be rejected by the body from which the original cell was taken. Here we have to distinguish between cloning of cells for medical uses on a patient and an entire cloned baby. Cloned tissue could be used for transplants, benefiting the patient and cutting down on animal experiments, but most people see the cloning of a new human being as unethical: an offence to human dignity – every individual should have the right to his or her own genetic identity – and potentially harmful to human genetic diversity.

Critics of human cloning are concerned that scientists are already working on creating a 'cloned person' – concerns not without foundation when in 1999 doctors in South Korea admitted that they had 'cloned the first human embryo'. The Christian Churches argue that human cloning:

- will interfere with diversity and could ultimately destroy the natural order
- will create psychological problems for the cloned child (for example problems of identity, and in relationships)
- will lead to a twenty-first century 'circus of human curiosities'
- smacks of scientists 'playing God' – leading to unpredictable and potentially devastating psychological problems.

Ethical issues arise too around the parental rights and responsibilities of the biological and the social parents, for example sperm donors and surrogate mothers. In 1984 the Church of England Board for Social Responsibility condemned surrogacy as violating 'the dignity of motherhood that a woman shall be paid for bearing a child'. IVF may also lead to the creation of 'spare' embryos, which can be frozen, donated for

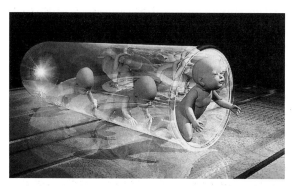

Fig. 5.5 'Human reproductive cloning is an offence to human dignity,' say opponents

research or allowed to die. It has also been questioned whether it is right to store an embryo until the mother (or someone else) decides to place it in the uterus and carry it to term.

For discussion

QUESTION: Is it right to change the DNA in sperm cells or ova and affect all future generations?

Yes. Failure to treat these cells will mean they are in any case transmitted to the patient's offspring.
No. At the moment we do not know that these techniques are safe enough to impose on future generations.

We can imagine some strange scenarios: Albert Einstein cloned from his brain cells, or a clone from the mummy of Tutankhamen. Have we the right to do such things? In fact, there is already a market for clones, though not human ones: the cloning of pets is already being attempted. But do not animals have rights to their own genetic identity too?

Everyone who is seriously involved in the pursuit of science becomes convinced that a Spirit is manifest in the Laws of the Universe - a Spirit vastly superior to that of man, and one in the face of which we, with our modest powers, must feel humble.

Albert Einstein, scientist

HUMAN IMPACT ON THE ENVIRONMENT

FOR more than a hundred thousand years, as long as human beings have lived in bands of hunter-gatherers, their impact on the environment was limited. But soon after the invention of agriculture around 7000 BCE and the resulting rise in human population came the first signs of environmental degradation due to humanity's activities. In central Jordan as early as 6000 BCE villages were being abandoned as deforestation was followed by soil erosion, which eventually degraded the landscape to the point where agriculture was no longer possible.

One of the first great civilizations of the world, the Sumerian culture of southern Iraq, was already in decline before 2000 BCE because of the deterioration of the soil and a decline in agricultural output. Sumerian civilization was made possible on the hot dry plains of Iraq only through the development of irrigation, but in summer high temperatures led to increased evaporation from the surface-water and a build-up of salt in the soil. At the same time water retention in the soil caused by poor drainage gradually led to waterlogging, and deforestation of the Turkish highlands caused increasingly large amounts of silt to be washed down to the plains and deposited on the land. The agricultural collapse was followed by Sumerian decline and invasion by Sargon of Akkad.

Once more in Iraq, 3000 years later, the brilliant Arab civilization of Baghdad supported a wealthy and sophisticated society. But again the pressure of population led to the same sequence of events: to boost food production canals were cut between the rivers Tigris and Euphrates, which led to waterlogging, a rising water table and a rapid increase in salination. The agricultural collapse which followed, together with the sack of Baghdad by Genghis Khan in the thirteenth century, led to the decline of the once-great Islamic civilization and opened the way to a period of European dominance.

It was only 300 years or so ago that the industrial revolution instigated a massive imbalance between humankind and nature. Although poets like William Blake (1757–1827) and Percy Bysshe Shelley (1792–1822) had the vision to warn people of the dangers of rapid urbanization, most people thought little about the polluting effects of industrialization on the planet. To the ambitious industrialists the earth's resources appeared to be infinite. However, in the 1960s, people began waking up to the devastating effects of two hundred years of industrialization and the Green Movement was born, challenging philosophers, scientists, theologians and businesses to consider **environmental ethics**.

ENVIRONMENTAL ETHICS ■

IN recent years moral philosophers have attempted to find an ethic that will guide us both communally and individually in our policies towards, and our treatment of, the natural environment.

Environmental ethics is a field of applied ethics concerned with issues arising out of human interaction with the environment; offering guidance about how people ought to think about the way they treat the environment; and seeking to evaluate past and present attitudes and practices.

The way we treat the environment today is deeply worrying and raises the question: is the environment simply an exploitable resource for human interests or has it significance independent of any use that might be made of it, a value that ought to constrain certain practices? Over the past twenty years the response to the environmental disasters facing us has included a number of different approaches:

a *Conservation ethics*. The planet and its ecosystem is not simply an end in itself but a *means* to ensure and sustain the well-being and continued existence of humankind and other life forms. This is the most common form of moral reasoning about the environment.

b *Non-human rights*. Rights have been extended to acknowledge non-human animals as well as humans. The Australian **ethicist** Pete Singer argues that to ignore other animals would be speceism (see page 60), and that 'the expanding circle of

moral worth' should include plants as well as humans and animals. This raises issues about how moral worth is related to consciousness. Ecologists such as Arne Naess, a Norwegian philosopher, have argued that all beings and objects that exist deserve moral status simply on the basis that they exist.

c *Eco-holism*. This view sees the inter-relatedness and interconnectedness of all things in the biosphere and geosphere of our planet. The **Gaia Hypothesis** (first put forward by James Lovelock in *Gaia: A New Look at Life on Earth*, 1977) takes the planet as a single and unified whole liable to gradual changes in its geophysical structure. According to Lovelock, human existence may be destroyed by Gaia's survival mechanism so that the environmental damage which threatens planetary survival will stop. Unlike religious systems the Gaia hypothesis seriously questions whether human life is dispensable in the great scheme of planetary survival.

For discussion

The earth will not be reduced to abject servitude. After all man's assaults, the majesty of the earth stands against him with an inscrutable countenance. There are gathering signs of a response in the form of massive retaliation. The game is a game but only if it leads to larger life. Else the game is no longer a creative experience but a struggle to the death, a struggle which man cannot win.

Thomas Berry,
modern geologist and theologian

Another approach is **Deep Ecology**, which teaches that the flourishing of human and non-human life has intrinsic value contributing to the realization of these values which are also values in themselves. It serves as the explanatory principle both for the pain we experience on behalf of our planet and its beings, and for the sense of belonging that arises when we stop repressing that pain and let it reconnect with our world. Deep Ecology draws on ideas found in the traditions of many First Peoples, expressed by the North American Indian Chief Seattle thus:

This we know. All things are connected like the blood which unites one family. Man did not weave the web of life, he is merely a strand of it. Whatever he does to the web, he does to himself. This we know. (Fig. 5.6)

In Central America, according to the Guatemalan Mayan vision of the cosmos, every form of life emerges from the same origin or seed. Some seeds become trees, others flowers, others human beings. Thus each creature is inextricably linked to all others, and what one does to a tree affects not only the tree, but oneself and other creatures. This interrelatedness calls for profound respect between people and their Creator, between people and nature, and among people themselves. The aim of the Maya is to keep their relationships with the world around

Fig. 5.6   To Native Americans all life is sacred

them in perfect balance according to the rhythms of the cosmos. No being is superior to another being, merely different, and from this springs the basic Mayan concept of unity within diversity. In the community all living beings are included, as each has their own unique contribution to make. Evil is recognized as part of reality and wrong-doing is punished so as to restore the equilibrium between the offender and the victim.

In eastern spiritual traditions, too, human interrelationship with creation is taught:

Those who verily depart from this world – to the moon, in truth they all go. During the earlier half it thrives on their breathing spirits (prana); with the latter half it causes them to be reproduced. This, verily, is the door of the heavenly world – that is, the moon. Whoever answers it, him it lets go further. But whoever answers it not, him, having become rain, it rains down here. Either as a worm, or as a moth, or a fish, or as a bird, or as a lion, or as a wild boar, or as a snake, or as a tiger, or as a person, or as some other in this or that condition, he is born again here according to his deeds (karma), according to his knowledge.

Kaushitaki Upanishad 1:2

Unlike many indigenous ethical systems, traditional western approaches to the natural environment have been strictly human-centred. The plight of the planet, ravaged by irresponsible human activity, demands a more holistic kind of ethic. This may mean that we stop regarding ourselves as superior to other life-forms. The Gaia Hypothesis suggests that our host planet is itself a huge, ruthlessly self-regulating biological organism. It is not committed to the preservation of human life at all. So it may be very much in our interest to convince our planetary host that we are worth keeping on as *environmentally conscientious house-guests.*

At present environmental ethics is in the process of evolution, with various strands emerging. Some theorists remain human-centred, some animal-centred, others promote a life-centred ecological holism. They range from utilitarian claims that humans need a healthy environment and so should take care of it, to discussions about the rights of rocks. Whatever approach is accepted the situation is serious, and many environmental ethicists argue that governments have a moral responsibility to adopt far-reaching measures now, before it is too late. These include:

- green taxation on businesses that abuse the natural world and exploit its inhabitants
- greater emphasis on corporate environmental ethics (see page 113)
- more research into alternative energy
- greater scrutiny of the nuclear power industry, particularly in solving the problem of nuclear waste as the atomic waste bill in Britain alone reached £355 million in 1998
- measures to reduce congestion and pollution from cars, and a rethink on road tolls and public transport
- a fairer distribution of resources; and more public scrutiny of the military-industrial complex that dominates the arms trade (see pages 110–11).

How long will this modern world last? If a hundred species of life can disappear in a month, if tigers have only five years left at this rate of killing, how long do we have? What can I do with a big car or marble house if in the process of mining metals for that car and blasting mountains for that marble, my air and water become unusable? A country should be measured, not by its gross national product, but by its grand national philosophy which keeps its citizens healthy and happy ... I turn my anger and grief into work, into daring to say that animal welfare is the key to human welfare, that compassion is an economic philosophy. I teach small lessons and big ones. This summer was a very hot one, and millions of birds dropped dead from the heat and from lack of water. This is also

watermelon time. I told my son we wouldn't eat watermelons, we'd put them out for the birds. We had hundreds of birds in our small garden. Watching them was a joy; they brought seeds of trees as gifts, which I put into pots and distributed in the neighbourhood. My garden is so full of trees that we are many degrees cooler than any other house I know. I just get my reward in the singing of the birds. I get it seeing my son mature. Animal abuse and environmental degradation are not necessary evils. No evil is necessary. Evil is present only as long as we support it. The moment we make the connection between what we know and how we behave, evil collapses. Mahatma Gandhi wrote: 'As human beings, our greatness lies not so much in being able to remake the world, as in being able to remake ourselves.' We need to remake ourselves as compassionate human beings. We need to learn and to teach the value of all life, because all life, not just human life, is sacred.

Maneka Gandhi, animal rights campaigner and former environment minister, India (1996)

Review

Generally, we can detect three distinct stages in humanity's attitude to the natural world:

- The attitude of native peoples the world over: the land is created and sacred, and all living beings should be treated with respect.
- The attitude of farming peoples: our land and our animals are our property, but still worthy of our respect.
- The attitude of the multinational companies, agribusiness, pharmaceuticals companies and biotechnological businesses: everything and everyone is a resource to be exploited; the bottom line is profit, not principle (see pages 112–13).

EXAM QUESTIONS

1 'Once fertilisation has taken place a new, unique human life, created by God, exists, and may in no circumstances be tampered with.' Do you agree with this view on embryo research? Give reasons.

[Oxford and Cambridge, 1996]

2 Discuss the ethics of transplant surgery.

[Oxford and Cambridge, 1997]

3 How does the use of animal organs affect the ethics of transplant surgery?

[Oxford and Cambridge, 1998]

4 Is Christianity necessarily 'green'? Defend your answer.

[Oxford and Cambridge 1998]

5 Does the present generation have an obligation to protect human life and the environment for the twenty-first century? Suggest what measures should be adopted now.

[Oxford and Cambridge 1997]

6 Outline what you consider to be the key issues in the debate between religion and science, and justify your views.

[EDEXCEL, 1997]

6 Sexual ethics

Sexuality is at the heart of the creative power of the universe. Every flower and blossom is a reproductive organ. The psychologist Carl Jung (1875–1961) stressed the creative power that is unleashed in human sexuality:

> The conflict between ethics and sex today is not just a collision between instinctuality and morality, but a struggle to give an instinct its rightful place in our lives, and to recognize in this instinct a power which seeks expression and evidently may not be trifled with, and therefore cannot be made to fit in with our well-meaning moral laws. Sexuality is not mere instinctuality, it is an indisputably creative power that is not only the basic cause of our individual lives, but a very serious factor in our psychic life as well ... Our civilization enormously understates the importance of sexuality.
>
> Carl Jung, *Psychological Reflections*

Popular approaches to sexual morality have argued for extramarital abstinence in purely consequentialist terms, from the fears of *conception*, *detection* and *infection*. Although contraception has greatly reduced the first fear, and social attitudes reduced the second fear, the Aids epidemic has led many to question issues around unprotected sex and promiscuity. In any case, consequentialist arguments, like utilitarianism, have limited ethical significance. They allow whatever good we want to maximize; but it is not at all clear that the new sexual freedom is necessarily the highest good. Utilitarians assume we can predict outcomes; but unforeseen and unwanted pregnancies still occur and thousands continue to be infected with the Aids virus in Britain and across the world (Fig. 6.1).

Meanwhile the problem of equal rights surfaces not only for broken relationships and the children of broken marriages, but also in women's ready access to abortion on

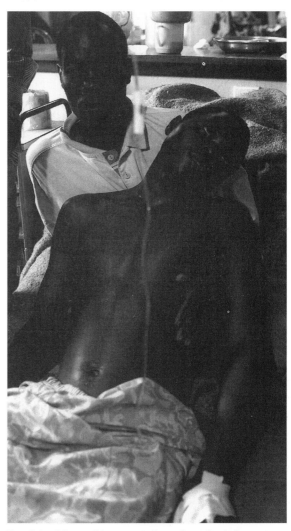

Fig 6.1 Many Africans infected with Aids cannot afford HIV drugs, which cost more than $560 a month. In Zimbabwe the average monthly wage is $37

demand. For the world religions the need for an ethic that goes beyond egoist and consequentialist approaches is imperative. Sex for individualistic ends can be manipulative, chauvinistic and a destructive power-play that ignores justice and love.

Many modern ethicists believe that current attitudes toward sex and marriage reveal 'a pervasive ethical egoism: in some cases Hedonism is at work, limited only by a harm principle reminiscent of Mill' (A. F. Holmes in *Ethics: Approaching Moral Decisions*, 1984). They argue that sex has become narcissistic and marriage merely a means to individual fulfilment. Husband and wife alike, in an individualism that can breed distrust and become destructive, have become means to each other's ends. Egoism, however, backfires because we naturally need and desire something other than our own satisfaction. World religions all teach that an adequate sexual ethic must recognize this, just as it must also insist on the equal dignity and rights of both men and women.

THE NATURAL LAW APPROACH

(see pages 26–7)

THIS is exemplified by the Roman Catholic Church's view, and sees sex as having a particular function – the procreation of children. Other uses of sex which frustrate this function are considered 'unnatural'. Many Christians today, however, disagree with such views and argue that same-sex relationships, if consummated with mutual and informed voluntary consent, can be as meaningful as so-called 'natural' acts. What is a 'natural' act anyway? Is heterosexual oral sex 'unnatural' because its prime function is not procreation?

St Paul first introduced the idea of celibacy to Christianity, cautioning that sex (along with other worldly pleasures) (Fig. 6.2) must not be all-consuming, and St. Augustine

Fig. 6.2   Detail from 'The Garden of Earthly Delights' by Hieronymous Bosch (c. 1507)

taught that humans need to renounce bodily pleasures if they are to achieve the higher ideal of contemplation. Sex was once pure and uncontaminated, but with the fall of Adam and Eve came original sin, interpreted as burning sexual desire tainted with evil; and original sin itself passes from one generation to another through sexual intercourse (thus, Jesus' birth by a virgin not through sexual intercourse ensured in Christian tradition that he was 'free from sin').

Celibacy was therefore confirmed by the Christian Church as the highest ideal, and sex within marriage regarded as a necessary evil for the continuation of the species. Such views influenced later thinkers in the Christian tradition – the general view being that sexual activity should only take place within the confines of marriage and that all sexual expression undertaken without human reproduction in mind – masturbation, anal sex, oral sex and the use of contraceptive devices – are 'unnatural' and therefore 'immoral'.

In the Old Testament the rite of circumcision was adopted as a sign that God's Covenant was with the children of Abraham for generation after generation. The genitals themselves were therefore to be a constant reminder that sexuality is God-given and that humanity is responsible in sex to God. Sexual union and reproduction were seen as being part of God's Creation, ordained in the institution of marriage. Sex is not to be treated in a purely biological and psychological fashion. Its ultimate meaning is not to be found in itself, in the act, the experience and even the social consequences. As with anything viewed spiritually, its ultimate meaning is to be found in *relationship*.

Christian ethics understands the psychology of sex as indicating its unitive potential, and the biology of sex as indicating its reproductive potential. In both cases the word 'potential' is stressed, for not every sex act is unitive, bonding a couple in mutual love and commitment. Sex can also alienate, degrade and dominate a partner, and by nature not every sex act can be biologically reproductive. But a sexual relationship has so plain a reproductive potential that childless marriages without planning are the exception.

Sexual attraction marks the beginnings of potential union, physically, emotionally, spiritually. The ongoing sexual relationship of a couple has the capability of nourishing love, expressing tender concern, eliciting honesty and trust, and renewing commitment. It can bind a couple ever more closely and firmly together. In its full realization it involves entire lives – the emotions, goals and values, the economic resources and social contribution of two people. It therefore defies egoism and points the way to mutual responsibility and service.

For discussion
- We engage in many activities unaccompanied by love or intimacy. Why should sex be any different?
- Cannot pleasure, without love and intimacy, serve as a legitimate goal of sex?

UTILITARIANISM ▬▬▬

(see pages 49–55)

UTILITARIANS view all sexual relations as acceptable if they take place in private (nobody else is involved or likely to be offended by it); the partners consent to it (it is considered by them to increase their own happiness); and it does not harm others. Although authoritarian and libertarian views are worlds apart they may well use the same utilitarian methods of assessing the situation. In recent years this has been highlighted by the advertising campaigns about contraception and the risks of HIV infection. The moral arguments in favour of taking a 'responsible' attitude to sex are utilitarian, and the shift in sexual attitudes brought about by the threat of Aids is largely due to the threat of harmful results; these can become the basis of 'responsible' behaviour on a utilitarian view.

Utilitarian arguments also surround issues around adultery and marriage. Often debate focuses not on the actual sexual desire of one person for someone who is not their marriage partner, nor on the morality of their sexual relationship as such, but on the potential harm that this might do to the emotional welfare of those damaged by infidelity, economic insecurity and deceit.

THE CONTRACTARIAN APPROACH ▬▬▬

RELATIONSHIPS are seen as being primarily about means by which individuals, whether heterosexual, lesbian or gay, can grow and develop in character and understanding through their contact with one another. The touchstone of whether a relationship is good or bad, and the criteria used for the assessment of sexuality, make little reference to traditional Christian views of no sex before marriage.

The Contractarian Approach emphasizes the importance of mutual, voluntary and informed consent, highlighting the appropriateness of tolerating sexual diversity as a recognition of human freedom and autonomy. Sex is morally permissible if, and only if, it is consummated with *mutual* and *voluntary informed consent*, without force, fraud and explicit duress. Therefore, sex is impermissible where one or both parties lack the capacities for informed consent (for example under-age, or significantly mentally impaired, or non-human); or where there is explicit duress (threats or extortion).

Although the contractual approach seems reasonable – a contract between people voluntarily agreed – this does not mean that the contract is *always* moral: one of the parties may be vulnerable, destitute or homeless, while the other may have more bargaining power. A middle-aged business-man can make a 'contract' with a 15-year-old homeless girl who is desperate for money. He can pass her money if she agrees to have sex with him. Although a contract (the passing of money) has taken place, such a contract is certainly not a moral one. Applying the Kantian principle (see page 44) ('It is morally wrong for persons to treat others merely as a means for their ends'), if one partner treats another as an object or manipulates them for their own purposes, or if the contract involves deception, force, exploitation or promise-breaking, it is wrong.

The Contractarian Approach can devalue sex because human sexuality is too personal and intimate to be reduced to a contract as if in a market place. Although people undertake a contract this does not always mean that both partners' long-term interests and happiness will ensue.

FEUILLETON FEMINISM ▬▬▬

MODERN feminists argue that it is *socially constructed sexual roles* that make it difficult for women to identify and nurture their own sexual desires and needs. Women are socialized to meet male sexual desires in order to prove their own value. Contractual arrangements are worthless because that same social conditioning that limits women's opportunities in the world will affect these so-called 'contracts'. Male dominance has influenced western sexual relations and women, politically victimized by their sexuality, will only be free from dominance when they are allowed the power and capacity to define themselves.

For discussion

The principle which regulates the existing social relations between the two sexes – the legal subordination of one sex to the other – is wrong in itself, and now one of the chief hindrances to human improvement and ... it ought to be replaced by a principle of perfect equality, admitting no power or privilege on the one side, nor disability on the other.

John Stuart Mill,
The Subjection of Women (1869)

Review

During the late twentieth century, modern popular thinking, influenced by developments in psychology, sociology and anthropology began to question traditional views, asking questions such as: why is sex within marriage for the purpose of procreation more in accordance with 'human nature' than sex outside marriage for the purpose of pleasure? This has not been an invitation to promiscuity but a view that sees sexual relations as being morally acceptable if love, trust, loyalty and intimacy are present. Such a view rejects mechanical and promiscuous sex as dehumanizing.

SACRED SEX AND INTELLECTUAL PERVERSION

WORLD religions have always recognized sexual love as a sacred gift. Modern culture however has person remains a sexual being, gifted by God for good. Our sexuality is expressed not simply genitally. It also finds expression in friendships and in the mutual contributions that we can make socially. Our highest good is not always necessarily found in sex or marriage, and both love and justice can operate to the full in other ways.

Jesus was single, and he observed that some people choose to be single for the sake of His kingdom (Matthew 19:10–12). St Paul noted advantages to singleness, benefits which he had undoubtedly experienced himself (1 Corinthians 7:32–5); and Roman Catholic priests take the Vow of Celibacy. The basic point is clear: both marriage and singleness find their meaning and purpose outside of themselves.

Homosexuality

In 1998 the Anglican Church voted that homosexuality was incompatible with Biblical teaching. Over recent years debate has raged about homosexuality within the Church. One of the most insightful views on this issue is provided by Desmond Tutu (b. 1931), the former Archbishop of Cape Town:

Among baptized Christians, members together in the Body of Jesus Christ, there is neither Jew nor Greek, male nor female, free nor slave. On the contrary, there is radical equality. But there are some we spurn and shun, because we are caught up in an acknowledged or tacit homophobia and heterosexism. We reject them, treat them as pariahs, and push them outside the confines of our church communities, and thereby we reverse the radical consequences of their baptism and ours. We make them doubt that they are children of God, and this must be nearly the ultimate blasphemy. We blame them for something that it is becoming increasingly clear they can do little about. Someone has said that if this particular sexual orientation were indeed a matter of personal choice, then gay and lesbian people
must be the craziest coots around to choose a way of life that exposes them to so much hostility, discrimination, loss, and suffering. To say this is akin to saying that black people voluntarily choose a complexion and race that exposes them to all the hatred, suffering, and disadvantages to be found in a racist society. Such people would be stark raving mad. It is only of homosexual people that we require universal celibacy, whereas for others we teach that celibacy is a special vocation. We say that sexual orientation is a matter of indifference, but what is culpable are homosexual acts. But then we claim that sexuality is a divine gift, which used properly helps us to become more fully human and akin to God, because it is this part of our humanity that makes us more gentle and caring, more self-giving and concerned for others than we would be without that gift. Why should we want all homosexual people not to give expression to their sexuality in loving acts? Why do we not use the same criteria to judge same-sex relationships that we use to judge whether heterosexual relationships are wholesome or not? I am deeply disturbed by these inconsistencies and know that the Lord of the Church would not be where his church is in this matter. Can we act quickly to let the gospel imperatives prevail as we remember our baptism and theirs, and be thankful?

Desmond Tutu in *We Were Baptised Too*

For discussion

'St Paul's teachings on homosexuality (see Romans 1:24–7; 1 Corinthians 6:9; 1 Timothy 1:10); towards women (see Ephesians 5:22–3; 1 Timothy 2:11–12); and the status quo (see Romans 13:1, 2; 1 Colossians 3:18–22) are irrelevant to the modern world.'

Look up the above references and discuss. Make notes and suggest to others in your class why these teachings continue to spark controversy.

Pornography

Pornography derives from the Greek *pornographos*, meaning *writing of harlots*, literally writing concerning or descriptive of prostitutes in their professions. Thus, the depictions of various forms of sexual intercourse on the walls of a certain building in Pompeii, intended as aphrodisiacs for the orgiastic parties (bacchanals) held there, were literally *pornographas*.

Pornography in this sense is identified by its sexually explicit content, its depiction of varied forms of sexual intercourse, turgid (swollen) genitalia, and so on.

> *The amount of explicit sex we see in cinemas has gradually increased. In Britain public tolerance of violence and particularly sexual violence is declining, while tolerance of sexual explicitness is increasing. We have no way of stopping cultural trends.*
>
> Andreas Whittam Smith,
> President of the British Board of
> Film Classification

Cultural trends – influenced by media technology (digital and satellite TV) and information technology (the Internet) – have meant that the British public has access to material that would not otherwise be shown in British cinemas. Films such as *Seul Contre Tous*, which won a prize at the Cannes Film Festival in 1999, would struggle to receive an 18 certificate in Britain because of a shot in a porn club showing images of penetrative sex and erect penises.

However, one person's 'obscenity' might be another's 'art'. Many cultures, although sharing the fundamental concept of the obscene, do not regard pornography, as defined above, as obscene. Some individuals may find copraphogy (eating faeces) obscene, but do not find pornography obscene, having different ideas about 'proper' sexual function and 'proper' excretory function.

If there is no necessary connection between the pornographic and the obscene, how did the connection between them arise? One account of the sexual morality behind this connection is that of the Catholic Canon Law which holds that 'Complete sexual activity and pleasure is licit and moral only in a naturally completed act in valid marriage'. This view derived from St Augustine's conception that the only proper 'genital commotion' is one with the voluntary aim of the reproduction of the species. Pornography is therefore obscene, not only in itself, because it displays intercourse outside marriage, but also because it tempts to intercourse outside marriage, or to masturbation, which are independently obscene acts because they are forms of sexual conduct that violate minimum standards of proper bodily function.

> *Pornography consists in removing real or simulated sexual acts from the intimacy of the partners, in order to display them deliberately to third parties. It offends against chastity because it perverts the conjugal act, the intimate giving of spouses to each other. It does grave injury to the dignity of its participants (actors, vendors, the public), since each one becomes an object of base pleasure and illicit profit for others. It immerses all who are involved in the illusion of a fantasy world. It is a grave offence. Civil authorities should prevent the production and distribution of pornography.*
>
> Catechism of the Catholic Church, 1994

While this Natural Law approach is not the universal basis for the connection of the obscene and the pornographic, this general view seems ever-present in Britain. Sexual function of certain rigidly defined kinds is only the correct and competent exercise of sexual function. All other forms, especially masturbation, are marked by failure, weakness and disgust.

This view is in part the result of obscenity legislation passed in Britain and the US in *physical or mental health of the pregnant woman greater then if the pregnancy was terminated or iii) that continuation of the pregnancy would involve injury to the physical or mental health of any coexisting children of the pregnant woman's family greater than if the pregnancy was terminated or iv) that there exists a substantial risk that if the child were born it would suffer from such physical or mental abnormalities as to be seriously handicapped.*

An increasing number of women today feel it is time to change the law again and remove power from the doctors in the first three months of pregnancy, thus allowing women to decide for themselves. The majority of women who seek abortion are not on the verge of a nervous breakdown as the media might sometimes lead us to believe, but are completely capable of incorporating a child into their lives. As rational beings they are quite able to make responsible choices such as delaying motherhood – so why in early pregnancy should they need two doctors' *permission*? There are also concerns that abortion is still regarded as an act that demands punishment and remains *stigmatized* in society. As well as questions around the law the abortion debate is an ongoing one and questions continue to be asked about the upper time limit of termination.

There is a part of the Abortion Act which refers to doctors who disagree with abortion on the grounds of conscience. Thus a doctor is fully entitled to refrain from giving advice about abortion or contraception if he or she has a **conscientious objection** to doing so. However, patients should be clear as to where they can seek advice if their own doctor does not deal with these areas of practice.

Technology

Since 1967 medical technology has made huge advances, and today ultrasound and computer graphics give us a window on the world of the foetus who, if necessary, can receive treatment in the womb. Babies can now survive, with a struggle, at 23 weeks. At the heart of abortion lies the question 'Why does a woman's right to reject unwilling motherhood carry more worth than the right to life of a foetus capable of survival outside the womb?'. This question was brought into focus in December 1998 with the news that a baby girl born at four months, weighing less than 420 g, had survived to go home.

Ethical controversy surrounds issues around **prenatal diagnosis**. This has particular reference to the abortion debate as many diseases and genetic disorders can be diagnosed before birth (for example through ultrasound imaging, when the foetus can be observed on the screen), thus giving the parents the choice of selective abortion. Other means of prenatal testing are invasive, for example amniocentesis or chorionic villus sampling. These methods carry a risk of injury to the foetus and sometimes induce miscarriage. These tests are usually only used when doctors suspect some abnormality, or if the mother is over 35 years old, or there is a previous family history of a genetic abnormality.

Many people involved in the disability movement are concerned that genetic screening means more and more disabled people need not be here at all. Organizations such as the British Council of Disabled People (BCODP) want to encourage more debate around the growing genetic drive to human perfection, and to raise public discussion about whether mothers have the right to abortion on grounds of 'foetal abnormality' (Fig. 7.1).

For discussion
- What are foetal rights?
- Who is the subject of the right to prenatal diagnosis – the parents, the child or society as a whole?
- Is a foetus a person, or a potential person?

Fig. 7.1 Disabled rights campaigners want to raise public awareness about whether mothers should have the right to abortion on grounds of foetal abnormality

Conflicting rights

As the parents are the creators of the child many people argue that parents have the right to prevent the birth or at least prepare themselves for any future difficulties that may arise. Yet these rights might be in conflict with the rights of the child or of society. Many women feel that any decisions that need to be made around abortion must take into account the role of the mother who has to go through the pain of labour and who is often primarily responsible for the nurturing of the child.

Feminists believe that women have *the right to choose* and, therefore, a woman's decision is paramount. Critics argue, however, that no rights are more important than the rights of another person to life, and that a foetus or embryo is a person. They argue too that a woman's rights, although needing to be recognized, cannot be considered in isolation; for example, what about a father's rights?

It is a fundamental principle in human society that life should be protected. Society, therefore, may exercise its right to defend and enhance life, sometimes independently of the wishes and interests of individuals. It may also interfere with actions of individuals if they have consequences which might be sufficiently costly to society. The birth of a child with spina bifida, for example, puts a heavy burden on public resources; by this reasoning, a state might consider itself to be justified in financing prenatal diagnosis and also, by extension, punishing cases of negligence leading to the birth of 'defective' children.

Scenarios such as these starkly illustrate the importance of the relationship between the law and medical ethics. Critics are worried that medical technology, in this instance prenatal diagnosis, encourages doctors and scientists to 'play God', arguing that natural processes should not be tampered with. A further concern about prenatal screening is the use of foetal tissue for genetic treatments. As a variety of genetic disorders are treatable by bone marrow transplantation, predictive genetic testing and tissue typing of foetal cells enable the parent(s) to know in early pregnancy that a foetus is genetically normal, and if this tissue matches a sibling with a genetic disease. Thus it is possible for a family to carry out a deliberate conception of a foetus in the possibility of providing tissue as a transplant donor.

Review

At what stage during pregnancy can a foetus be regarded as an individual? This question has perplexed theologians, philosophers and medical ethicists down the ages. Indeed, the way we answer this question will influence our views on other issues concerned with medical ethics. The key questions are: Is a foetus a person, or a potential person? Has a foetus rights, and if so, how are these rights to be balanced against the rights of the mother? Is the foetus a person at sixteen weeks when it begins to move, or is it a person only at 34 weeks when it is developed enough to live outside its mother's womb?

Roman Catholic teaching

'Thou knowest me right well; My frame was not hidden from thee When I was being made in secret' (Psalm 139). The Psalmist considers that God's interest in the individual is evident from the earliest moments of life, a theme echoed in Jeremiah: 'Before I formed you in the womb I knew you' (1:5). If life in its fullest sense is imbued with meaning, even from its first form, then to interfere or destroy it is wrong. In the Birth Story in Luke's Gospel there is an awareness of the significance of the foetal Christ when the Angel Gabriel tells Mary that even before he is born God has a plan and purpose for the child still in the womb.

At the heart of abortion lies the question 'Is a foetus a person, or a potential person?'. St Augustine maintained that the soul was implanted by God at 46 days, whereas Thomas Aquinas maintained that the souls of girls were implanted at 90 days and the souls of boys at 40 days. Abortion, therefore, was not a problem provided it was carried out before the soul was 'implanted'. In the seventeenth century, however, the Roman Catholic Church taught that God *implanted the soul at the moment of conception*, which led to the Catholic view that all abortion is murder and embryo research is unacceptable. Four basic principles summarize the Roman Catholic theological position on abortion:

- God is the Lord of life and death – a person's ultimate value stems from God and no individuals can take it upon themselves to place themselves in total mastery over the life of another.
- Human beings do not have the right to take the lives of others: 'Thou shall not kill' (Fifth Commandment).
- Human life begins at the moment of conception.
- Abortion, at whatever stage of development of the foetus, is the taking of human life.

But does the Church accept that in some complex cases 'indirect abortions' are acceptable? These are normally dealt with under the 'principle of double affect' which holds that some actions are so evil that they can only be permitted if some other aim was sought – for example, a pregnancy may terminated if its likely consequence is the death of the mother.

The publication in 1140 of Gratian's *Decretum* was the first fully systematic attempt to compile ecclesiastical legislation on abortion. He maintained the distinction between formed and unformed foetus, and argued that it is not murder to abort a foetus before the soul is in the body.

Up until the sixteenth century the Church followed a tradition which did not treat as murder the killing of the embryo under 40 days. Even if it was destroyed after 40 days it was not regarded as murder because it was rarely killed in hatred. However in 1588 Pope Sixtus V abolished the traditional distinction between formed/animate and unformed/inanimate foetuses and called all acts of abortion 'murder' in his Papal Bull *Effraenatum*. In addition, anyone who had anything to do with abortion was excommunicated. However, Pope Gregory XIV revised this, stating that only those who aborted an animated foetus would be excommunicated.

In the nineteenth century the number of abortions being carried out increased significantly. The Church reacted and Pope Pius IX stated that Mary was free from sin 'in the first instant of her conception' – all references to the distinction between inanimate and animate dropped. The embryo was regarded as being inviolate with independent integrity. In 1930 Pope Pius XI issued his encyclical *Casti connubi* which spoke of 'the most grave crime of which the offspring hidden in the maternal breast is attacked'; 'the killing of the innocent'; and that 'the life of each is sacred'.

During the 1960s the Second Vatican Council (1962–5) decided that 'abortion and infanticide are abominable crimes' and that 'life must be safeguarded with the utmost care from the moment of conception'. In

1968 Pope Paul VI in his encyclical on birth control, *Humane Vitae*, again declared that 'the direct interruption of the generative process already begun, and, above all, directly willed and procured abortion, even for therapeutic reasons, are to be absolutely excluded as licit means of regulating birth'.

Pope John Paul II reaffirmed the fundamental theme of the inviolability of human life from the moment of conception, arguing that the denial of the right to life of the newly conceived undermines the entire fabric of Christian ethics:

> *Human life must be respected and protected absolutely from the moment of conception. From the first moment of his existence, a human being must be recognized as having the rights of a person among which is the inviolable right of every innocent life.*
>
> Catechism of the Catholic Church

The Pope recognized that the decision to have an abortion is often a tragic and painful one for the mother, often made not for selfish reasons nor out of convenience, but out of a desire to protect certain important values such as her own health, or a decent standard of living for other members of the family. However, these reasons, however serious or tragic, can never justify the deliberate killing of an innocent human being. Direct abortion, willed as an end or as a means, always constitutes 'a grave moral disorder', since it is the deliberate killing of an innocent human being. This doctrine, the Pope maintains, is based upon Natural Law (see pages 26–7) and upon the written Word of God which is transmitted by Church tradition (see pages 34–8).

Protestant teaching

In November 1998 a doctor who performed abortions was shot dead in his home by a member of an anti-abortionist group. Many such groups exist in the USA, with strong links with Protestant fundamentalist groups and **Christofascists**. They argue that the foetus is a human person from conception, which itself is an act of God: 'Whatever therefore God has joined together, let no person put asunder' is, for fundamentalists, a Biblical principle applicable to the abortion debate. They usually agree that the foetus may be terminated when the life of the woman is at stake.

Not many Christian groups, thankfully, undertake such murderous acts to drive their point home. The Church of England, for example, has committed much time and energy into trying to find an acceptable resolution to the dilemmas of abortion and acknowledges that the foetus, a potential life, has a significance which cannot be overlooked, minimised or denied. Much debate within the Church has centred on weighing the claims of the mother against the claims of the foetus, or vice versa, when they conflict, recognizing that neither mother nor foetus must be thought of in isolation from the family group within which they exist.

Generally, the Church of England believes that all human life, including life developing in the womb, is to be protected; and expresses serious concern about the large numbers of abortions carried out under the current legislation. It also recognizes that there are situations in which abortion is justified (namely the risk of a defective or deformed child and in cases of incest and rape). Some members of the Church, however, would limit abortions only to life-threatening situations while others would permit them for emotional or socio-economic reasons. The Church desires to find a right course of action which (although it might not be perfect) corresponds to the circumstances people find themselves in. Abortion is an evil, but it may in some circumstances be the lesser of two evils.

In general, the Protestant position embraces the following principles:

a Life is to be preserved rather than destroyed.

b Those who cannot assert their own rights to life are especially to be protected.

c There are exceptions to these rules, including:

  i when 'medical indications' make therapeutic abortion morally viable

  ii the pregnancy has occurred as the result of a sexual crime

  iii the social and emotional conditions do not appear to be beneficial for the well-being of the mother and the child.

For discussion

What is crucially important is compassion for the woman involved, and her ability to make a humane decision grounded in freedom of choice. Some people argue that abortion has allusions with war; as the morally conscientious soldier fighting in a particular war is convinced that life can and ought to be taken, 'justly' but also 'mournfully', the moralist can be convinced that the life of the defenceless foetus can be taken, less justly, but more mournfully.

Review

The Fifth Commandment 'Thou shalt not kill' (Exodus 20:3) stresses the sanctity of life and, traditionally, for many Christians, expresses the last and final word on abortion. However, it is disputed whether those engaging in abortions are of murderous intent because often motives of compassion and concern drive people to advocate and/or practise abortion.

EUTHANASIA

THE term euthanasia comes from two Greek words – *eu*, meaning 'well', and *thanatos* meaning 'death' – and means 'painless, happy death'. Some definitions broaden this to mean 'termination of human life by painless means for the purpose of ending severe physical suffering', or 'mercy killing'. If human life begins at the moment of conception and ends at the moment of death, and humans have a right to be treated as beings worthy of respect throughout this period, then the unborn child or the unconscious adult should be protected in exactly the same way as a conscious adult. In this respect abortion and euthanasia are often linked, and the ethical basis for this position has been the Natural Law approach to ethics (see pages 26–7).

Voluntary euthanasia

Any justification of voluntary euthanasia (the request and consent of the dying person) is generally made on the grounds that death is preferable to the suffering that would be involved if the person continued to live. In other words, it is based on *expected results* (relief from anticipated pain). This may be related to the pain, physical or emotional, that the patient may be experiencing, or the suffering of family and friends which the patient seeks to avoid. Most groups currently campaigning for changes in the law to allow euthanasia are campaigning for *voluntary euthanasia*, i.e. euthanasia carried out at the specific request and consent of the dying person. The Voluntary Euthanasia Society (EXIT) campaigns so that:

> *An adult person suffering from a severe illness, for which no relief is known, should be entitled by law to the mercy of a painless death, if and only if that is their express wish ... Doctors should be allowed to help incurable patients to die peacefully at their own request. The patient must have signed, at least 30 days previously, a declaration making their request known.*

Involuntary euthanasia

This is when someone is killed in order to save them from additional suffering, but when in spite of being capable of consenting to their own death they do not do so, either because they are not asked, or because when asked they choose to go on living.

Suicide

This is self-administered euthanasia. Although suicide is not illegal some people consider it to be morally wrong. Assisting someone to commit suicide is illegal.

Non-voluntary euthanasia

This is the killing of someone who is not in a position to ask to live or die (for example newborn babies, or a person severely brain-damaged and in a long-term coma). When discussing cases of non-voluntary euthanasia there is often a dispute as to when death actually occurs. Traditionally, death was seen as occurring when there is a permanent cessation of the functions of both the heart and lungs. However, modern technology (especially respirators) has provided doctors with the means to maintain the functioning of the patient's heart and lungs after they have ceased to function naturally. In some cases heart and lung function can be restored or continued by artificial means even after brain function has been partially or completely destroyed.

Some definitions of death state that the loss of functioning of the whole brain is required for death – whole brain death. Other definitions include brainstem death – the part of the brain responsible for the physiological and anatomical core of human life, where loss constitutes the death of the human being as a whole. Upper brain death/ death of personhood defines death as the permanent absence of consciousness, thought and feelings, which are seen as being necessary for personhood.

Active and passive euthanasia

In practice euthanasia involves either:

- passive euthanasia – allowing someone to die by withdrawing treatment, for example turning off a life-support system to which a comatose patient has been connected; or

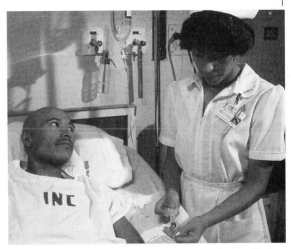

Fig. 7.2 Under British law a person has the right to refuse treatment as long as he or she is fully competent to make such a decision

- active euthanasia – something is done actively to end life, for example in time of war, a mortally wounded soldier in great pain may ask his comrade to 'finish him off' in order to shorten his suffering.

Because medical technology is advancing all the time the ethical issues around euthanasia are more complex than ever before. Under British law a person has the right to refuse treatment as long as he or she is fully competent to make such a decision (Fig. 7.2). If a person is not in a position to ask for or refuse treatment then a doctor can decide to withhold treatment.

A 'Living Will'

In the Netherlands, euthanasia, although not strictly legal, is widely practised, accounting for about 8% of all deaths; and in the US a patient can make a **'Living Will'** which sets out the conditions under which he or she wishes to die. The suggested wording is:

If I should have an incurable or irreversible condition that will cause my death within a relatively short time, and am no longer able to make decisions regarding my medical treatment, I direct my attending physician . . . to withhold or withdraw treatment that only prolongs the process of dying and is not necessary to my comfort or to alleviate pain.

Autonomy

One of the cornerstones of medical ethics is autonomy (i.e. the right of the patient to decide his or her own treatment) – the patient has the right to choose the timing of his or her own death. Doctors are faced with the difficulty of deciding whether a patient is mentally alert enough to make this decision. The fact that patients may feel pressured to accept assistance in a premature death in order to relieve anxious relatives of financial pressures or emotional strain are concerns that need addressing. Another important consideration both for the individual and for society at large concerns how we rationally allocate resources. The cost of dying takes up large amounts of money in health care spending. Could money spent in sometimes futile intensive care treatment be better spent in other areas of health care?

The Book of Job

Despite enduring terrible calamities ('chastened on a bed of pain'), The Book of Job describes Job as refusing to take his own life, arguing that the human race must accept suffering just as we accept happiness and joy. This life is only meaningful when we view it in a larger picture. Life is short but we are free to find meaning, even in the midst of all our troubles.

Compassion

Compassion is at the heart of Jesus' teachings ('Love your neighbour as yourself') and those who call themselves Christians are called to try and follow his example. The problem as regards euthanasia is that it is not always clear what the most compassionate action is – obviously the alleviation of pain is important, but if this is only to be achieved through the taking of life what is the most ethical way to act?

A Roman Catholic view

In his 1995 encyclical *Evangelium Vitae* Pope John Paul II confirmed earlier positions of the Roman Catholic Church:

> *Euthanasia is a grave violation of the law of God, since it is the deliberate and morally unacceptable killing of a human person.*
> *This doctrine is based upon the natural law and upon the written word of God*

The Pope teaches that human life has a unique value in the whole of creation, it is an *extraordinary gift* which is defended by the Commandment 'You shall not kill' (Exodus 20:13).

However, some modern Christian theologians argue that active euthanasia is acceptable if it preserves a person's freedom and dignity when threatened by an agonizing illness or if it is born out of compassion and love for the person suffering.

Ethical theory

Euthanasia thus illustrates the ethical division between Natural Law arguments (see pages 26–7) and those based on Situation Ethics (see pages 47–9) which argues that a person should do whatever love requires in a particular situation, and that may mean helping to end a life.

Other theologians argue against active euthanasia because:

- they believe the legislation of voluntary euthanasia would create a precedent to extend the practice to disabled and sick people who are a 'burden' on society – the danger of escalation
- mercy killing could destroy the fundamental value of trust between patient and physician

- of the difficulties in defining the 'free consent' of the patient
- euthanasia could have a harmful effect on society – as long as human dignity is not

based simply on usefulness to society, people such as the mentally ill, the severely handicapped, the very sick must be treated with respect.

EXAM QUESTIONS

1 Explain and evaluate the differing attitudes to abortion. [Oxford and Cambridge, 1997]

2 'Abortion is an issue which is concerned *only* with rights and duties.' Discuss.
[EDEXCEL, 1998]

3 Examine the distinctive contribution religion makes to the debate on two of the following issues:
  (i) euthanasia
  (ii) aided conception
  (iii) the use of animals in medical research
  (iv) tolerance of homosexual relationships.
[NEAB, 1998]

4 Why are there differing Christian views on the subject of voluntary euthanasia? Suggest ways in which these attitudes might be reconciled.
[Oxford and Cambridge, 1998]

5 Should Christians view euthanasia as unacceptable in all circumstances?
[EDEXCEL, 1996]

6 'The case for euthanasia bears no theological, philosophical or social justification.' Discuss.
[Oxford and Cambridge, 1996]

8 *Human rights*

THE STRUGGLE FOR A UNIVERSAL ETHIC

THE struggle for a Universal Ethic has been an ongoing feature of humanity's attempt to create a global moral order where peace, justice and equality prevail worldwide. One of the drawbacks of some modern approaches to human rights concerns the method of presenting them as a code of civil and moral laws, and perhaps as a product of western civilization, when in fact human rights are essentially a codification of mainly spiritual laws that are themselves the cumulative achievements of the world's religious traditions, East and West.

CULTURAL RELATIVISM

CULTURAL relativists see moral beliefs and practices as varying with and depending upon the human needs and social conditions of particular cultures, so that no one moral belief-system can be universally true. There can be no universal 'oughts'. In studies of both primitive and modern cultures anthropologists have found that variations can exist in terms of customs, moralities and beliefs from culture to culture. This observation – that different cultures have different moral codes – has provoked some philosophers to conclude that there is no such thing as one universal 'Truth' in ethics and, therefore, we cannot judge different cultures to be 'correct' or 'incorrect' because this would imply that we have an independent standard of right and wrong (by which they may be judged). Cultural relativism, however, poses some fundamental problems.

Firstly, in theory, cultural relativism is the reasonable idea that certain social, economic, cultural and political practices are inherent to particular groups and that the abrupt, artificial introduction of alien influences can be disruptive. In practice, however, cultural relativism is often employed by ruling elites as a pretext for opposing reform movements that threaten their power or status. Thus, calls for the respect of basic human rights are dismissed by politically motivated relativists as culturally insensitive or socially impracticable. Such claims can conceal crude anti-foreign nationalism.

While each individual, each society, each cultural or ethnic entity, may have its own definition or understanding of human rights, these rights are often used as a pretext to preserve systems that guarantee power to those resisting the implementation of universal human rights. The issue, of course, is the manipulation of power, which is how many view politics today. In fact, 'politics' in its true sense should mean 'community building.' A politics based on the manipulation of power can only succeed if people unquestionably accept cultural relativism, whereas community building can only lead to cooperation, social harmony and constructive activity.

Secondly, it does not necessarily follow that because different cultures have different moral codes there is no objective moral truth. The conclusion 'no objective truth in morality' does not logically follow from the premise 'different cultures have different moral codes'.

Thirdly, cultural relativism adopts a tolerant attitude towards other cultures. This sounds fine, but what if another society practises a barbaric act – like female circumcision for example? In principle a cultural relativist, believing there are no absolute truths in ethics, would have to sit back as young girls are mutilated, and would not be in a strong position to condemn a society that practises female circumcision. In the nineteenth century, practices such as slavery in the USA or child labour in Britain were common. Today such practices are outlawed. We call this progress. However, progress means replacing certain practices and attitudes with *better* ways. If the old ways agreed with the social standards of the time, then cultural relativists would say it is mistaken to judge them by the standards of a different time.

Lastly, many factors contribute to produce the customs and moral beliefs of a society, not least religious beliefs. It would be wrong to conclude that simply because customs differ there is disagreement about *values*. In some Muslim societies men are allowed to marry more than one wife, whereas in cultures dominated by Christianity men have only one wife. Both groups, however, Muslims and Christians, believe that women, like men, have rights and are made in the Divine Image. We cannot conclude, therefore, that just because customs differ there is necessarily disagreement about basic *values* such as the belief in human dignity regardless of gender or race. These values *are* universal. For example it is wrong to take another human life. Imagine a society where murder was not condemned – it would be total chaos.

> **Review**
> Despite its problems, cultural relativism can prevent people from assuming that all their morals are based on some absolute standard and, therefore, cannot be questioned – a view which can lead to dogmatism, fundamentalism and fascism.

CULTURAL ABSOLUTISM ▬

CUTURAL absolutists maintain that ultimate moral principles do *not* vary from culture to culture. This does not mean that all cultures have the same moral rules and *prescriptions* but that *ultimate principles underlying all the various rules and prescriptions are the same*. A cultural absolutist might argue that all cultures have the same underlying principles, for example to value human life or to protect the young. Although there are many different prescriptions that ensure that this be done, the underlying value remains the same.

The Golden Rule

If we look at some teachings from the sacred scriptures of the world religions we find some 'core principles'. Despite differences in cultural beliefs and customs there are some underlying ethical principles that, although arising in different cultures and at different periods of history, are identical. History records that from age to age Enlightened Ones have imbued the human race with a profound consciousness imparting a new significance to all aspects of life including art, government, education, science and architecture, relating individual life to a Higher Purpose.

Underlying the astounding diversity of traditions that have developed over the centuries there lies a common foundation manifested in cosmological, eschatalogical, and theological teachings about human origins and destinies. This underlying unity is exemplified in the ethical systems of different faiths, especially in the teaching that we should treat others as we ourselves would wish to be treated (the Golden Rule).

> **The Golden Rule**
> *Therefore all things whatsoever ye would that men should do to you, do ye even so to them: for this is the law and the prophets.*
> Gospel of Matthew – Christian tradition

> *Do not to others what ye do not wish*
> *Done to yourself; and wish for others too*
> *What ye desire and long for, for yourself*
> *This is the whole of the Dharma.*
>
> *Mahabharata* – Hindu tradition

> *What is hateful to you, do not do to your*
> *   neighbour;*
> *that is the entire Torah; the rest is*
> *   commentary.*
>
> *Talmud* – Jewish tradition

> *Since to others, to each one for himself, the*
> *self is dear, therefore let him who desires*
> *his own advantage not harm another.*
>
> *Udana-Varqa* – Buddhist tradition

> *None of you truly believes until he wishes*
> *for his brother what he wishes for himself.*
>
> *Hadith* – Islamic tradition

> *If thine eyes be turned toward justice,*
> *choose thou for thy neighbour that which*
> *thou choosest for thyself.*
>
> *Kalimat-i-Firdawsiyyih* – Bahá'í tradition

Natural rights

The Greek philosophers through to St Aquinas argued that there is a Natural Law which underpins the order of the universe. This order can be understood through the power and application of reason. Philosophers such as Thomas Hobbes and John Locke used this idea of Natural Law to establish some basic and 'natural rights', which include the right to life and personal freedom. However, some modern philosophers have rejected these 'natural rights', arguing they are not self-evident (for example there is no self-evident object in existence called 'equality').

Christianity and other religions believe, however, that because life is created the natural right to life is attached at birth, or even prior to birth. Human rights are in effect the right of an individual to fulfil his or her God-given calling freely, without obstruction by others. The right to be treated as a person is then the right to the responsible life God has purposed for us.

Rights and duties

We have rights such as free speech, which means we should be left free from interference. We also have rights to certain provisions, for example the right to a living wage (something that should be provided). When I have a right, therefore, somebody else, or other people, or the authorities, have a duty to leave me alone or provide the service I claim. If a person claims a legal right, then this entails a duty on someone to see that this right is respected. Such is the basis of all contracts, and all legislation which protects particular rights.

> *Whatever is my right as a man is also the right of another and it becomes my duty to guarantee as well as to possess.*
>
> Thomas Paine (1737–1809), political writer, *The Rights of Man*

HUMAN RIGHTS

HUMAN rights, although having their roots in spiritual traditions, have evolved alongside moral, social and political agreements made between human beings – enshrined in public documents, authorized by international communities and entrusted to a worldwide organization to ensure that such rights remain sacrosanct. The term 'human rights' is relatively recent, and it has become a twentieth-century name for what has been traditionally known as 'natural rights' or 'the rights of man'. Their roots can be found in such ancient texts as the Babylonian Code of Hammurabi and the juridical rulings of the Jewish Sanhedrin, which banned torture and limited the use of capital punishment.

The Universal Declaration of Human Rights

No culture can be adequately understood without an understanding of the religion that underlies it – the culture of a society is 'the society as spirit'. It is the 'spirit' of a society that can recognize human rights as a code for upholding the dignity of the human being. The Preamble to the Universal Declaration of Human Rights states emphatically that the purpose and aim of the Declaration is a profound belief and firm faith in:

The dignity and worth of the human person and recognition of the inherent dignity and of the equal and inalienable rights of all members of the human family is the foundation of freedom, justice and peace in the world.

Embedded in the Preamble is a principle akin to Kant's Practical Imperative (see pages 42–7): irrespective of race, creed or colour all persons are deserving of respect. Although there is widespread acceptance of the principle of human rights, domestically and internationally, there is not complete agreement about the nature of such rights or their definition. Some of the most basic questions have yet to receive conclusive answers. Are human rights divine, moral, or legal entitlements? Are they to be validated by intuition, custom, conscience, and social contract theory? Are they principles of distributive justice or prerequisites for happiness? Are they to be broad or limited in number and content? These are matters of ongoing debate and will remain so as long as there exist contending approaches to public order and scarcities among resources.

The Universal Declaration of Human Rights is an inspiring, poetic and visionary document. Adopted by the United Nations in 1948, it continues to dominate contemporary discussions on human rights. The French jurist René Cassin was the principal author of the document, and found the source of the rights he proposed in civic, moral, legal and spiritual traditions. The Declaration continues to throw out a moral challenge to all those in power today. Despite the fact that 117 countries still practise torture and a new refugee appears on Earth every 21 seconds, there is a growing realization that people are global citizens with universal rights: 'All human beings are born with equal and inalienable rights and fundamental freedoms'.

For discussion

Article 1 of the Universal Declaration of Human Rights states:

All human beings are born free and equal in dignity and rights. They are endowed with reason and conscience and should act towards one another in a spirit of brotherhood.

The right to freedom of thought, conscience and religion

One of the most controversial of the declarations is Article 18, which states that everyone has the 'right to freedom of thought, conscience and religion', including freedom to choose and change religion. This includes in its language both humanistic and religious dimensions. Today Article 18 continues to be flagrantly violated in many parts of the world.

This is starkly illustrated by the severe repression of members of the largest religious minority in Iran, the Bahá'í community. The Bahá'í faith is one of the world's newest religions. Founded in the mid-nineteenth century by Baha'u'llah (1817–92), its earliest followers faced persecution at the hands of state authorities. Over the next century the Bahá'í faith grew both inside and outside its Iranian homeland, but the 1979 Islamic

Revolution in Iran resulted in massive violations of basic human rights for Bahá'ís. The Bahá'í have never, individually or collectively, advocated violence and are enjoined by their own ordinance not to participate in politics. Persecution reached its height in the 1980s with attacks and executions of individual Bahá'ís and the destruction of shrines, cemeteries, homes and businesses. Only when Bahá'ís recanted their faith and converted to Islam could their rights as citizens be restored.

Another example can be found in Tibet, where the invading Chinese have slaughtered tens of thousands of Tibetans and destroyed more than 6000 of Tibet's temples and monasteries. The Potala Palace, which lay at the heart of Tibetan religious culture, has become little more than a tourist attraction as China deliberately, brutally and systematically continues to annihilate a culture permeated by a profound spiritual tradition.

In India, too, concern is growing over the persecution of Christian minorities by Hindu fundamentalists (Fig. 8.1).

Any exploration of the relationship between human rights and religion needs to acknowledge that religious bodies have a dismal history on the issue of human rights, as have many secular institutions. In the 1990s the world watched on TV the atrocities in Bosnia-Herzegovina where men who called themselves Christians carved crosses on the cheeks of yet-living Muslim men before killing them. We do not have to search very deeply into contemporary history to find variations on this pattern: Muslims murdering Christians; Hindus killing Muslims; Christians killing Jews, and so on, seemingly *ad infinitum*. As religious distinctions are often motivating factors in numerous ethno-political conflicts, the charge that religion is a great source of violent conflict cannot be denied.

That institutionalized religion has fuelled so much fanaticism and hatred has led many to conclude that it is out of date and no longer applicable to the needs of modern life.

In the late nineteenth century Friedrich Nietzsche proclaimed the 'death of God' (see pages 40–1), thus helping to create the intellectual climate that led many people in the twentieth century to lose faith in God and adopt a bleak view of humanity's place in the universe.

In the modern age 'religious truth' has been questioned and the principles of scientific determinism, Marxism, **Freudianism**, capitalism and materialism have been valued over those of the spiritual, reducing us in the process to the plaything of economic and social forces. Yet to act on this judgement brings its own evils and will do nothing to advance the cause of justice and peace. Carl Jung analysed the consequences of the loss of religion when he observed that spiritual traditions:

Fig. 8.1 Indian Christians protest in Delhi after sustained persecution by Hindu extremists

... express the whole range of the psychic problem in mighty images; they are the avowal and recognition of the soul, and at the same time the revelation of the soul's nature. From this universal foundation no human soul is cut off; the loss of this great relationship is the prime evil of neurosis.

Prisoners of conscience

During the First World War conscientious objectors, realizing the futility of the war, refused to fight. Often they were ridiculed, persecuted and even killed for their beliefs. The freedom to be allowed to follow the 'dictates of conscience' is a fundamental human right. However, this right is constantly being violated by different political systems across the world. Sometimes, confronted by the cruelty provoked by such violations, Christians and non-Christians alike have spoken out. Sometimes they are severely punished for this. In modern times many individuals, acting according to the dictates of conscience (see pages 27–32), have come into opposition with the ruling authorities.

Today many people are imprisoned for following their conscience, and organizations like Amnesty International campaign for the release of these prisoners of conscience. One example is the case of Mordechai Vanunu, an Israeli nuclear technician. In 1986 Vanunu gave information and photographs to *The Sunday Times* to alert the world to the dangers of Israel's extensive secret nuclear arsenal. He was abducted by Mossad, Israel's Secret Service, and in a secret trial convicted of treason and espionage and sentenced to eighteen years in prison. Since then he has been held in solitary confinement under harsh conditions amounting to torture. Apart from his lawyer, only immediate members of his family are allowed to see him once a month in the presence of a prison officer. In 1996 he went on hunger strike after losing his appeal against solitary confinement. As Vanunu is not prepared to remain silent he is unlikely to be released in the near future. In his defence Vanunu was reported as saying: 'I'm not a traitor. I'm a man with a conscience who did what he did out of a deep belief, after much thought and many doubts.'

Torture and repression

In 1996 the Asylum and Immigration Act in Britain was passed, severely limiting people from applying for asylum. The applicants are usually people fleeing from political tyranny and torture. Many critics of this Act think the British government makes life intolerable for those who apply or who appeal against the Home Office decision to refuse their claims. The Medical Foundation for the Care of Victims of Torture and Action by Christians Against Torture (ACT) work to help such people.

The degree of callousness in our society concerns me – the ease with which the homeless, the single parent, the asylum seeker become scapegoats for all the ailments and insecurity of our society. The devaluation of a group of people so different from ourselves that it doesn't matter what happens to them is what leads to persecutory thoughts and behaviour. I have an abhorrence of people who torture their fellow human beings. But it is the states which allow and in some cases actively encourage its practice which preoccupies me more. And it is the bystanders amongst us who alarm me almost as much as the torturer. This may sound strange, but I have accepted that an enemy of humanity exists, an evil that one has to work against, but the bystander is someone who knows what is going on and does nothing. If we look at the latter part of

Americans are 'God's chosen people'. They can also be described as Christofascists. One of their preachers has been reported as saying: 'Adam was white. Noah was white. Jacob was white and Jesus was white. And God sent the white man to America to establish the true religion and American Constitution, govern the heathen and institute righteousness. The white man in America was ordained to be the last stronghold of His righteousness' (quoted in E. Vulliamy, 'White supremacy unmasked', the *Guardian Weekend*, July 1998). Racism goes to the heart of our society today (Fig. 8.2), something that a leading police chief, David Wilmot, acknowledged in 1998 when he said of the British police force:

There are a range of issues that go from overt racism, such as verbal abuse, physical abuse or antagonistic behaviour, down to internal racism that affects the way you deal with individuals or situations.

David Wilmot, *Police Review*

Fig. 8.2 Racism goes to the very heart of society

The public admission of racism in the police force was unprecedented and was welcomed in the black community. But doubts continue to grow about the legal system in the wake of the death of the black teenager Stephen Lawrence, who was murdered by white racist thugs in 1993. The reaction of the rank and file of the police, however, shows how much progress still has to be made. Many police officers were angry. They say they are not racist. Many black people disagree. There is obviously a gap between the perceptions of both groups, and this in itself indicates that something is very wrong.

The Police Federation argues that the police force is no more racist than society at large, but commentators say this is not good enough: the police have to be *better* than society at large. An article in *Black Perspective* (1998) made the point: 'After all, one can confront a racist neighbour, or fight the National Front, but how does a young black man stand up against a racist policeman?'

The Macpherson Report (1999) into the death of Stephen Lawrence stated that 'pernicious and **institutionalized racism**' played a crucial part in failing to bring Stephen's murderers to justice. The police stood accused of institutionalized racism, which for many black people is confirmation of what they have known and experienced for years, namely that the police are predisposed to treat black people like crooks when they are the actual victims of crimes. Macpherson stated that institutionalized racism was prevalent in the investigation into Stephen Lawrence's death; in the huge disparity in stop and search figures nationwide 'which points to a clear core conclusion of racist stereotyping'; in a significant under-reporting of racial incidents due to lack of confidence in the police; and in the failure of police training. The report stressed that racism, institutionalized or otherwise, is a disease that affects other agencies in society, including those dealing with housing and education.

THE RIGHT TO LIFE

And you shall hallow the Jubilee year and proclaim liberty throughout the land to all its inhabitants ... And if your brother becomes poor, and cannot maintain himself with you, you shall maintain him ... Take no interest from him or increase, but fear your God; that your brother my live beside you.

(Leviticus 25:10, 36)

There is a 'New Slavery' in the world today, a slavery which keeps Africa, Asia and Latin America crippled by debt payments. Twenty-five million children will die this year because of debt (Fig. 8.3) and millions more will grow up unable to read or write as government budgets for health and education are dwarfed by debt repayments to the West. The inherent instability and injustice of economic globalization has led many people to join Jubilee 2000, a coalition of 70 aid agencies, trade unions and churches who campaign to write off foreign debt.

Fig. 8.3 Twenty-five million children will die this year because of debt repayments

EXAM QUESTIONS

1 To what extent can a human being have rights without corresponding duties?
[EDEXCEL, 1997]

2 Discuss the relation between the rights and responsibilities of citizens.
[Oxford and Cambridge, 1996]

3 Should social obligations restrict individual rights? [EDEXCEL, 1996]

4 Explain to what extent, if at all, the problems associated with poverty may be met by the social ideal of equality.
[Oxford and Cambridge, 1997]

5 'Religious principles do not guide believers to the right decision. Rather, they allow believers to justify almost any action in the name of their faith.' Discuss this statement, illustrating your answer with reference to *two* moral issues.
[NEAB, 1997]

McDonald the clown. Despite UK Advertising Codes forbidding commercials which 'manipulate the emotions of children', the provocation of what is known in the industry as 'pester power' is widespread. *McDonald's Operation Manual* reads: 'Ronald loves McDonald's and McDonald's food. And so do children, because they love Ronald. Remember children exert a phenomenal influence when it comes to restaurant selection. This means that you should do everything you can to appeal to children's love for Ronald and McDonald's.' Geoffrey Guilano, the actor who played Ronald the clown in the 1980s, eventually resigned saying 'I brainwashed children into doing wrong. I want to say sorry to children everywhere'.

For discussion

A consumer society, by offering objects one buys as the ultimate adventure to the young, is subtly eating away at the soul of the young and its potential for great things and great visions.

Matthew Fox, modern theologian

Exploitation

As well as exploiting the minds of children, McDonald's stood accused of exploiting rainforests, animals and employees (Fig. 9.1). It was alleged that in South America every year an area the size of Wales is stripped of virgin rainforest to provide land upon which the global beef market, of which McDonald's is the world's largest single user, can indulge its appetite for low-cost cattle. It was alleged too that hens providing eggs for McDonald's Egg McMuffins are kept in battery cages with no access to sunlight and less than the size of an A4 sheet of paper as space for each bird.

Critics of McDonalds also state that many 'McJobs' employees of McDonald's find themselves in poorly paid dehumanizing work devoid of employment rights. Sid Nicholson, McDonald's UK vice-president, admitted that for staff aged 21 or over, the corporation 'couldn't pay any lower wages without falling foul of the law'. McDonald's has allowed no trade unions, and once in Canada ordered its employees to lie down in the snow to form the word NO, affirming the corporation's paranoid view of trade unions. Such an attitude to trade unions could be seen as a violation of the UN Declaration on Human Rights, which states that: 'Everyone has the right to form and to join trade unions for the protection of their interests' (Article 23:(4)).

For discussion

The love of money is the root of all evil.

1 Timothy 6:10

Fig. 9.1 McDonald's stood accused of exploiting rainforests, animals, employees and customers

THE NEW GLOBALISM

ACCORDING to the United Nations, multinational companies now control more than 70% of world trade. Names such as ICI, General Electric, McDonald's, Nestlé are known from the shantytowns of Beijing and Bombay to the leafy suburbs of Bristol and Boston. These business organizations control production, investment and marketing, and decide what jobs are located where, what working conditions prevail and what living conditions are possible. An increasing number of people fear that the power of multinationals to manage production on a global scale, and their readiness to leap national borders in search of higher profits, laxer laws, and lower costs, threatens democracy itself.

The corporations themselves often use the word 'globalization' to describe how the world economy has been transformed in recent years. They would like to see all barriers and regulations that might impede the free flow of capital or restrict the operations of the market place dismantled; investors allowed to put money where they think the biggest profits are irrespective of ethical implications; manufacturers allowed to sell their goods where prices are highest; and labour prepared to move to where wages are highest.

Globalization, however, creates enormous problems. As soon as corporations are free to move across borders but labour is not, massive unemployment occurs in countries 'left behind'. When capital and goods are internationally mobile then capital will tend to seek a low-cost labour work-force, leaving higher-cost labour on the scrapheap.

Globalization produces common experiences all over the world. For example, Manjeet worked for nine years as a home worker making baby clothes, receiving 20p for a dress and 90p for a christening gown. She earned one pound an hour and worked 12-hour days. Working alone at home, she was isolated and unable to find other homeworkers with whom to discuss work conditions and pay. She does not live in Asia, but in Yorkshire. The National Group on Homeworking (NGH) estimates that there are at least one million homeworkers in the UK, many earning as little as 30p an hour. 94% of homeworkers are women.

> *The history of our time has shown in a tragic way the danger which results from forgetting the truth about the human person. Before our eyes we have the results of ideologies such as Marxism, Nazism and fascism, and also of myths like racial*

> *superiority, nationalism and ethnic exclusivism. No less pernicious, though not always as obvious, are the effects of materialistic consumerism, in which the exaltation of the individual and the selfish satisfaction of personal aspirations become the ultimate goal of life. The rapid advance towards the globalization of economic and financial systems also illustrates the urgent need to establish who is responsible for guaranteeing the global common good and the exercise of economic and social rights. The free market by itself cannot do this, because in fact there are many human needs which have no place in the market.*
>
> Pope John Paul II, *Fides et Ratio* (1998)

HISTORY OF BUSINESS ETHICS

BUSINESS ethics, like medical ethics, tries to apply general ethical principles such as rights and responsibilities to rather specific and often unique situations. However, while doctors enjoy professional status, business people on the whole do not – society tends to see their motives as driven by greed (**avarice**) rather than any higher goals. Although business ethics as currently practised is an increasingly important area of ethical investigation, it was Aristotle who first distinguished two different practices involved in business: firstly, household trading (*oikonomikos*), which he approved of; and secondly, trade for profit (*chrematisike*), which he felt was immoral. Those who engaged in such practices were according to Aristotle nothing more than 'parasites'.

This distaste of usury (using money with the sole intention of making more) and of profit-making was around right up to the seventeenth century, highlighted by Shakespeare in his depiction of Shylock in *The Merchant of Venice*. Prior to this the Gospels record Jesus as driving the money-changers out of the Temple in Jerusalem, and Christian moralists from St. Paul to Thomas Aquinas and

Martin Luther (1483–1546) often condemned what we call today 'the business world'. However in the sixteenth century John Calvin (1509–64), the Swiss Protestant church reformer, taught the virtues of thrift (using money wisely and carefully). The Freemasons adopted a code which influenced good business practice:

A Mason is particularly bound never to act against the dictates of his conscience. Let a man's religion or mode of worship be what it may, he is not excluded from the order, provided he believe in the glorious architect of heaven and earth, and practise the sacred duties of morality.

By the eighteenth century the world was changing fast. Agrarian societies gave way to urban, larger, more centralized societies. With the advance of technology and the growth of industry Aristotle's *chrematisike* became the central institution. The Scottish economist Adam Smith (1723–90), in *The Wealth of Nations*, advocated individual enterprise and free trade. Industrialists such as Andrew Carnegie (1835–1919) gave lectures on the virtues of success and the obligation of the rich to help the poor; while business ethics as a discipline tended to become a **socialist** critique against the immorality of slave labour and the division of labour.

It is only recently that the idea of studying the underlying values of business has taken on new momentum. Ethicists are no longer primarily concerned with just criticizing business and business practice, although this is still a key element, but are asking questions about *responsibility*.

For discussion
There is no vice more detestable than avarice.

Plato, *Republic*, III, 42

You cannot serve God and Mammon.

Jesus, Matthew 6:24

BUSINESS AND ETHICS

Business Ethics, as a discipline, can be broken down into three areas:

a Micro-ethics – the rules for exchange between individuals. Micro-ethics in business relates to the nature of promises, intentions, consequences, obligations and individual rights; the idea of fair exchange and fair wages and fair treatment.

b Macro-ethics – 'the business world' consisting of cultural or institutional rules of commerce for an entire society. Macro-ethics relates to large questions about justice: What is the purpose of the free market? Is it 'fair'? Is it 'efficient'? How do we define efficient? Does it pay enough attention to need? What is the role of government? Are private property rights primary or just one ingredient of the market?

c Molar-ethics – relates to the social, environmental and personal responsibilities of the powerful minorities who control business: directors and owners of the huge corporations which dominate the modern business world.

For discussion
It is difficult but not impossible to conduct strictly honest business. What is true is that honesty is incompatible with the amassing of a large fortune.

Mahatma Gandhi

Social responsibility

The injustices perpetuated by the modern global marketplace make sober reading. Microsoft Corporation makes £20 million profit a day. This is what sub-Saharan Africa pays each day in debt service (interest on capital repayments). The £16 billion Britain is spending on 232 new Eurofighters would cancel the entire debt of sub-Saharan Africa and south Asia. Much of the debt is related to arms sales and the arms trade. Britain is the third largest exporter of weapons, and over the past ten years more than a quarter of the UK's debts have come from arms supplies. In 1996 Britain sold sixteen armoured combat vehicles and seventeen Hawk aircraft to Indonesia, where half the population does not have access to sanitation and the Indonesian government has invaded East Timor, murdering 200,000 people. Brutal and corrupt regimes are the biggest customers as they need sophisticated weapons to keep themselves in power.

Philosophers and members of the public are naturally suspicious of enterprise, and the first task of business ethics has been to clear the way through the incriminating myths so that the underlying ethos that makes business possible on local and international scales may be properly understood.

'Business myths'

- *Business is just about profits.* The profit motive, something of which business executives are proud, was in fact a phrase coined by nineteenth-century socialists as an *attack* on the narrow-minded pursuit of money to the exclusion of all other considerations. Although businesses obviously still strive for profit today, this is only part of the picture, as it is acknowledged that businesses also supply goods and services and provide jobs and work within a community. However, multinational corporations, arms manufacturers and agrochemical companies are less attached to local communities or even to their country of origin, and as loyalty fades so does responsibility. When you buy a meal at McDonald's, less than a quarter of the money you spend stays in the local area.

  The operation of a business is dependent on society and businesses have responsibilities. Business must benefit not only those who create it but also those who permit it, namely society as a whole. Bribery, profiteering, coercion, rationalization, falsification of records, corporate espionage and tax evasion are irresponsible and all violate the social contract, as do pollution, sexism, racism, urban blight, slave labour and exploitation. Many multinationals continue to violate such principles in their pursuit of the global market, although they are able to get away with it because there are, as yet, not enough legal restrictions to stop them. The principle known as the Iron Law of Responsibility tries to counter such malpractice, and states that those who misuse power should lose it, and if they contribute to social harm they have a proportional obligation to contribute to its alleviation.

- *Business is dog eat dog.* Business is often viewed as cut-throat, 'the law of the jungle', the 'survival of the fittest'. However, business also rests on a foundation of shared interests and mutually agreed rules of conduct, with competition taking place within some sort of community which business both serves and depends upon, relying on networks of suppliers, service people, customers and investors.

- *Business is about everyone for himself or herself.* This is often referred to as atomistic individuation: the idea that business life consists wholly of transactions between individual citizens. This may have been the case in eighteenth-century Britain, but today business life often involves governments (by way of subsidies, tariffs, taxes, etc.) and is a social practice and not just the activity of isolated individuals. One of the most dominant models of modern business is corporate culture, which recognizes the place of *people* in the organization and acknowledges that only shared values, as opposed to individualism, can hold a corporate culture together. This might be fine for those in power within the corporation, but workers are easily thrown into unemployment in the ruthless pursuit of lower costs.

For discussion

In the eyes of Jesus, money takes its place among the demonic powers which enslave men. That is why he gave it a demonic name, Mammon *(Matthew 6:24; Luke 16:13).*

J. J. Von Allen, modern French theologian

Stockholders and stakeholders

In 1970 the economist Milton Friedman (b. 1912) wrote a controversial article in *The New York Times* in which he said: 'the social responsibility of business is to increase its profits'. He argued that businessmen who believed in corporate social responsibility were deluded because managers of a corporation have a responsibility *only* to their stockholders – giving money to charity or funding community projects was akin to 'stealing from the stockholders'.

Friedman's views are extreme but nevertheless influenced the British Prime Minister Margaret Thatcher in the 1980s. Since then businesses have tried to change their image and transform the idea of 'stockholder' to 'stakeholder'; stakeholders being employees, consumers, suppliers, the surrounding community and society at large. Social responsibility is seen as part and parcel of a corporation's essential concern, to serve the needs of, and to be fair to, not only investors or owners, but those who work for, buy from, sell to, live near, or are indirectly affected by the activities of the free market system. However in practice such principles are not always adhered to.

Supermarkets

Molar-ethicists are increasingly concerned that the Big Four British supermarket chains – Asda, Safeway, Sainsbury's and Tesco – are abusing their monopoly of the food retailing sector. Farmers ask what has

Fig. 9.2 Supermarkets stand accused of unethical business practices

happened to the £45 million difference between what they get for their meat at the market and what it was sold for in the shops. Supermarkets are being accused of:

- *forcing* their suppliers to make donations to charity in their names
- *profiteering* and squeezing their supply chain by not passing all of their savings to the consumer (Anne Perkins, 'The price is wrong', in the *Guardian*, January 1999)
- *rationalizing* their supplies; aiming to have no more than three suppliers of any commodity, from cauliflowers to carrots
- *destroying* traditional high streets – the number of independent food retailers has halved in ten years, from 400,000 to 200,000, squeezed out by the impact of the chains; superstores cost on average 270 local jobs;
- *sneaking* genetically modified foods (see page 68) on to their shelves without labelling them as such.

PROFIT BEFORE PRINCIPLE

MANY corporations today pollute the environment with toxic chemical wastes; produce lethal or unsafe products; discriminate against women or minorities; bribe government officials; buy and sell companies to plunder their products; and throw the work force into unemployment and slavery. They are among the most blatant violators of the UN Declaration on Human Rights.

Specific examples abound: the deadly chemical accident in Bhopal, India in 1984 which blinded thousands of people and killed thousands more when poisonous gas escaped from a factory owned by the US company Union Carbide (Fig. 9.3); enormous oil spills into the pure waters of the sea by ships like the *Exxon Valdez* and the *Sea Empress*, which leaked 70,000 tonnes of crude oil along the Pembrokeshire coast of Wales in 1996. Today Mexican border towns are garbage dumps for millions of barrels of benzine solvents, pesticides, raw sewage and battery acid, spewed out by the 1,800 foreign-owned companies based in Mexico because of its cheap labour. These companies also dump toxins into landfills, rivers and drains, and millions of gallons of toxic waste are dumped daily into the Rio Grande in Texas. Along the Mexican Pacific coast an estimated 1000 gallons of poisoned water pours into the ocean every *second*. The result is high incidences of brain haemorrhages and lung, liver and kidney damage amongst the local communities.

Milton Friedman contends that corporations cannot meaningfully be said to be 'persons with responsibilities'. But he fails to acknowledge a basic premise: *no citizens can have rights without corresponding responsibilities*; and a person, whatever position he or she holds in a corporation, is an agent who makes decisions and acts, and is held morally responsible for those decisions and actions. Friedman has also been criticized for arguing that a corporation that fails to maximize its profits has broken its promises to its shareholders. However, no such 'promises' are actually made, and even if they were, a 'promise' can be overridden by more important moral concerns. Friedman argues that the management is the agent of the individuals who own the corporation, and as such it has a duty to maximize profits. But management often does not act like an agent and actually in some cases ignores the wishes of shareholders.

Perhaps the most undervalued stakeholder within a capitalist economy is the employee. In traditional free market theory, the employee's labour is itself just one more commodity subject to the laws of supply and demand. Today multinationals with no sense of responsibility or obligation to local communities can make thousands of people unemployed overnight as they cross new frontiers into countries in the poor South – particularly Africa, South America and India – in pursuit of lower costs.

Fig. 9.3 Irresponsible business practices result in disasters like this one in Bhopal, India

For discussion

Capitalism claims that the single-minded pursuit of profits by organizations as a means of charting a straight course for what is best in society (which seems to be a utilitarian one: the greatest good for the greatest number) can be achieved only if corporations act solely in the pursuit of profit and ignore moral concerns. But will a selfish society in which everyone pursues self-interest turn out to be better than a society in which people are regulated by a sense of moral responsibility to others?

Advertising

The managers of corporations, enjoying the *rights* of the free market, have *responsibilities* too. These obligations include obvious ones like ensuring their products are safe but also less obvious obligations involving advertising. The classic defence of the free-market system is that it supplies and satisfies existing demands. But if manufacturers actually create that demand for the products they make, then their classic defence is undermined.

Some macro-ethicists argue that advertising is coercive (it forces itself upon potential consumers) and interferes with the free choice of consumers who become subject to a barrage of influences which may well be quite irrelevant or even opposed to their real needs. Although raising many serious ethical issues advertising is a worldwide, all-pervasive phenomenon.

But simply because it is legal, is it morally acceptable to use sex to enhance the appeal of products from chocolate bars to cars? Should advertisers be allowed to present implied but deviously false promises of social success and acceptability if one buys their product? Is advertising a lie when it implies that a certain pair of jeans will guarantee that 'you'll pull'? Are products, especially medicinal ones, sold under false pretences especially when some products have unpleasant side effects? Is it right that adverts promise things they cannot possibly deliver, such as popularity and respect, creating a consumer itch that cannot be scratched? Is it right that in a world in which many people are struggling financially, advertising encourages people to want more and more? Is it right that advertising portrays an 'ideal', built around looks, youth, glamour and material possessions – things that don't last – and that short-term gratification rules? Is it right that in a world of hungry people adverts encourage greed, to want more things – to hog the world's resources for ourselves? Do adverts deliberately try and make us feel inadequate when we don't look like the young 'dude' in his high-fashion clothing or the 'babe' on a desert island eating chocolate?

The media

The fact that powerful individuals can monopolize newspapers, advertising, satellite television, film and publishing and override human interests in pursuance of political and economic aims is a source of concern for macro- and molar-ethicists.

They are also concerned about the effect that advertising can have on people's minds: compared with 1950 we are substantially more depressed, and today's 25-year-olds are about ten times more likely to suffer from depression then their grandparents. Similar scales of increase have occurred in rates of violence and gambling.

Critics of current business practice argue that the fundamental cause of this deterioration in our well-being is the outbreak of 'keeping up with the Joneses' through envy, long regarded as one of the **seven deadly sins** by Christians. The media, by deliberately *overstimulating our instinct to rank ourselves against each other*, encourages dissatisfaction with what we *have* got, creating a longing for *new* commodities, *new* jobs, *new* bodies, *new* partners, and even *new* identities to make us feel better. The critics believe that this 'psychic holocaust', caused by the myth that both our material lives and our inner lives will be improved by consumption, is a lie driven by business as it continuously looks for increased profits, new markets and economic growth.

Business ethicists argue that a radical alternative to this view is necessary if we are to achieve the Good Life in its truest and fullest meaning. We need to learn that *economic growth, wealth and possessions do not lead to happiness*. With more equitable distribution of wealth and less stimulation of our competitive-comparative instincts at the expense of cooperative, altruistic ones, we could begin to concentrate on making a world fit for future generations.

Censorship

The film industry has discovered that sex and violence sells. But do such portrayals have harmful consequences? If people are offended by sexually explicit films or 'video nasties' should these films be banned?

Critics of **censorship** argue that people who are offended by sexual or violent portrayals have a choice – they can switch off. They also argue that a diet of sex and violence does not alter or affect people's behaviour. However, history has shown that some films do lead to certain people acting out their fantasies in real life (e.g. 'Birth of a Nation' glorifying the Ku-Klux-Klan (see pages 103–4) in America and Hitler's propaganda films in Germany led to an increase in racially motivated attacks by racist thugs). Violent behaviour triggered by watching a film is something we would recognize as harmful consequence.

For discussion

While the controversy and debate continue, the body of literature that has grown out of psychological research supports the view that there is a link between violence in the media and violent behaviour among children.

Roger Hock, psychologist
Forty studies that changed psychology

Violent actions are generally wrong; unnecessary violence is always wrong. As a general principle, if an action is morally wrong it is always wrong to depict it in a way that implies that the action is condoned, or even worse, approved of. Thus the wrongness of certain actions seems to provide a built-in reason against depicting these actions *gratuitously* (in an unnecessary or undeserved way). Explicitly violent films treat bodies as objects and people as mere disposable commodities, with the watcher

remaining detached and not really entering into someone else's experience. It is *what* they suffer that is important, not *that* they suffer. Even if we know that the victims of violence are actors, and the violence is created by special effects, the suspicion is that the watcher takes an interest in the special effects because he is interested in the effects themselves. What about behaviour triggered by watching sexually explicit films? Perhaps films with elements of both sex and violence will increase the incidence of rape, but will a man be driven to rape as a result of watching sexually explicit, 'hard core' films?

In the same way that some violent films treat people as objects, some sexually explicit films treat bodies as objects. Sexual intercourse involves an intimate relationship between two people; as soon as an audience is introduced the situation changes. A watcher, or voyeur, is not part of that interpersonal relationship, and if they are aroused at the sight of others' love-making they are aroused not as the lovers are – by an interaction with the other person in the relationship – but by what the two people are doing to each other. The love-making couple are then perceived merely as objects. Some people argue that films made simply as vehicles for the sex, and which contain scenes of explicit sex solely for the purpose of attracting and stimulating a larger audience, exploit, demean and undermine the intimate and creative power of human sexuality. This view is held by both the Catholic and Protestant Churches.

For discussion

Viewing people as objects leads to treating people as objects, because how we view people determines how we treat them.

A censor is an official who examines printed matter, films, or sometimes in war, private letters, with the power to remove anything

War and peace

WAR

WAR is defined as armed hostilities between peoples, frequently different nations, sometimes between different parties within a nation, as in a civil war, or between one small group and the state, as in a guerrilla war. The supposed aim is for one group to win by inflicting maximum damage on the other with minimum damage to itself, an aim only modified when there is a need to preserve some of the enemy as slaves or peasant workers. However, to a passing alien from another world, this apparently rational aim-oriented activity might appear simply as a baffling process of reciprocal destruction.

Traditionally, war did not directly involve civilians if they were not in the way, but in 1937, during the Spanish Civil War, the city of Guernica was bombed from the air, including both civilian and military targets, and since then the entire populations of contending countries have been in the front line. During the Second World War 55% of casualties were civilians, yet in the 1998 war in Sudan 97% of casualties were civilians.

Although war is often glamorized on television and in films, in reality it is a dirty business. When the Americans waged war in Vietnam in the 1960s their express desire was not to kill the enemy but to 'incapacitate' as many civilians as possible (Fig. 10.1) and by so doing put intolerable pressure on hospital and health facilities. Rather than bury her, it takes time, resources and energy to attend to a 12-year-old Vietnamese child with napalm burns all over her body. Many have questioned, too, the ethics of the great bombing raids of the Second World War, when British and American bombers rained down fire and destruction on millions of German women and children, and the use by the Americans of atomic bombs in Japan.

Today the problem is even greater, as nuclear, biological and chemical warfare are capable of eliminating not just combatants but the entire human race. In a world brimming with such dangerous weapons, we have to ask what are the causes of war, and how can its dangers be controlled, and if possible eliminated? At one time individuals like Alexander and Rameses II were given the title 'the Great' for slaughtering human beings on the battlefield, but today few would view the killing of vast numbers of non-combatants for no rational purpose as anything other than a crime against humanity.

Throughout history human beings have been fighting, maiming and killing each other. The reasons they have given for

Fig. 10.1 The Americans dropped napalm bombs on Vietnamese civilians to *incapacitate* as well as *incinerate*

taking another human life have been many: duty, honour, dignity, king/queen, country or God. For followers of world religions, often caught up and involved in conflict, war poses fundamental questions about human worth and dignity. The German Protestant reformer Martin Luther, alluding to the story of Samson in the Old Testament, suggests that few of us are in any position to decide another person's fate, let alone take his or her life:

You ask, Why may I not use the sword for myself and for my own cause, with the intention by so doing not of seeking my own interest, but the punishment of evil? I answer, Such a miracle is not impossible, but quite unusual and hazardous. Where there is such affluence of the Spirit it may be done ... No one but a real Christian and one who is full of the Spirit will follow this example. If reason also should follow this example, it would indeed pretend not to be seeking its own, but this would be untrue. It cannot be done without grace. Therefore, first become like Samson, and then you can also do as Samson did.

PACIFISM ▰▰▰▰▰▰

A **PACIFIST** is a person who is opposed to war and violence. Pacifists believe that it is wrong to harm or kill other people, and that if killing is wrong, then war must be wrong, as war is basically a matter of killing. The English philosopher Bertrand Russell pointed out that 'patriots always talk of dying for their country, but never of killing for their country'. War means killing and inflicting suffering on other people, but do we have the right to do these things? If we apply the Golden Rule ('Do to others as you would wish them to do to you') we have to ask if we would like to be shot or gassed, if we would like to see our grandparents bombed, or our children burned to death in a firestorm created by carpet-bombing.

Many people argue that war is sometimes necessary to protect our family and fellow-citizens, or to defend our ideas of freedom, justice and peace. But pacifists ask how can war protect peace, how can killing preserve freedom, how is justice preserved by the evils of war? Pacifists are often asked, 'What would you have done about Hitler?' and they reply that it is necessary to resist evil by non-violent means, always retaining a reverence for life. For if we abhor Hitler because he was a mass-murderer, how can it be right for us to murder women and children in bombing raids in order to defeat him?

For discussion

... all who take the sword will perish by the sword.

Matthew 26:52

Pacifists believe in the 'sanctity of life', arguing that war conceals the basic truth of the kinship of humankind by defining certain groups as 'enemies' rather than as fellow human beings. Albert Camus (1913–60), the Algerian-born French writer, said: 'We are asked to love or hate such and such a country and such and such a people. But some of us feel too strongly our common humanity to make such a choice.'

Enemies are defined by governments and can change from day to day. At the beginning of the Second World War the Russians were enemies of Great Britain, as they had signed a pact with Hitler to carve up Poland between them. In 1941, however, Germany invaded Russia, and suddenly the Russians were our allies. After the war, relations between east and west deteriorated, and the Soviet Union once again became an enemy, or a potential enemy, of ours, and then after the collapse of communism and the break-up of the Soviet Union in the early 1990s the Russians once more became our friends. Then the west found a new enemy in the Iraqi president Saddam Hussein, although before the invasion of Kuwait by Iraq he was regarded as a friend by the British and US governments.

It is often said that 'The first casualty of war is the truth', and at the opening of the Gulf War a Kuwaiti princess appeared on TV to tell the world how, when Iraqi troops had taken over a hospital in Kuwait, they had disconnected the life-support machines for premature babies. This was a lie. At the beginning of the First World War it was reported that when the Germans had invaded Belgium they had raped Belgian nuns and forced them to ring church bells to celebrate the German victory. Millions of young men in Britain and the Commonwealth volunteered to kill Germans on the strength of such reports, although it was only after the war that they found out that this too was untrue, a case of 'Chinese whispers' starting with a newspaper report that the Germans had forced a priest to ring the bells.

For discussion

The first casualty of war is the truth.

Pacifists believe that war and violence are inhumane, impractical, immoral, unjust and wasteful. In place of violence they offer non-violence, understood not just as the avoidance of violence, but as the active search for positive ways of solving conflicts and achieving real peace. Pacifists point to the success of the non-violent campaigns led by Gandhi and Martin Luther King, regarding their approach as more moral and humane. Pacifists renounce war, and in times of conflict they may become conscientious objectors, join the ambulance service or fire service or work as hospital porters. Many Quakers (members of the Society of Friends), in both world wars, joined the ambulance service and cared for the wounded and dying on the battlefield, a job which required as much courage as any soldier's.

Pacifists may engage in educational work to spread their ideas; they may take part in demonstrations; they may refuse to pay taxes to buy armaments (an organization called *Conscience* campaigns for the right for people to be able to choose to have the military part of their taxes spent on peace-building alternatives); or they may practise other forms of civil disobedience and work to improve society and remove the causes of war – repression, exploitation, injustice. They try to break the vicious cycle of selfishness, greed and violence which breeds war and revenge. To do this they say we must start by examining our own responsibility for the violence that exists in the world. Most of us would say we believe in the 'Brotherhood of Man', in the sanctity of life, and perhaps even in loving our neighbours as ourselves. Yet, according to Tony Augarde in *Peace is the Way* (1990), as soon as our government tells us that somebody or other is now our enemy we allow fear and unreason to get the better of us, a red mist descends before our eyes, and we find ourselves shouting 'Kill the Germans ... Russians ... Iraqis ... '.

The Quakers and absolute pacifism

George Fox (1624–91), the founder of Quakerism, believed that the same living Christ who appeared in the Scriptures as a historical figure was also present in the inner world of human beings as a source of universal love and spiritual guidance. The Christ was not just present in the historical Jesus, but is present as a seed in the heart of the individual, and manifest as the Inner Light which guides his or her actions. As there is 'that of God' in every person, George Fox believed in the 'Brotherhood of Man', as all are children of one common Father. He utterly rejected war as being incompatible with the teachings of Jesus:

We utterly deny all outward wars and strife and fightings with outward weapons, for any end or under any pretence whatsoever. And this is our testimony to the whole world. The spirit of Christ, by which we are guided, is not changeable, so as once to command us from a thing as evil and again to move unto it; and we do certainly know, and so testify to the world, that the spirit of Christ, which leads us into all Truth, will never move us to fight and war against any man with outward weapons, neither for the kingdom of Christ, nor for the kingdoms of this world.

Declaration of the Society of Friends (Quakers) to Charles II (1661)

Christianity and pacifism

In seventeenth-century England, the Quakers taught an uncompromising pacifism, and remain to this day strong supporters of the pacifist movement. The Christian pacifist alternative to the politics of power is to create conditions for social justice, enabling the poor to free themselves from the oppression of moneylenders and landlords; to devote resources to meeting human needs instead of the stockpiling of weapons of mass destruction; to build bridges between communities creating trust and respect, and to develop non-violent strategies for resolving conflicts. Even Pope John Paul II, not usually thought to be a pacifist, has eloquently expressed the pacifist position:

Violence is a lie, for it goes against the truth of our faith, the truth of our humanity. Violence destroys what it claims to defend: the dignity, the life, the freedom of human beings. Violence is a crime against humanity, for it destroys the very fabric of society ... To all of you who are listening I say: do not believe in violence; do not support violence. It is not the Christian way. It is not the way of the Catholic Church. Believe in peace and forgiveness and love, for they are of Christ.

Christian pacifism has its roots in the life and teaching of Jesus himself. Though the Old Testament often saw God as the 'Lord of armies', directing the wars of Israel, Jesus identified himself with another strand of Old Testament thinking, found in the vision of the Prophet Zechariah, of a Messiah who would banish chariots and war-horses and 'speak peaceably to every nation'. Jesus took the part of the suffering servant of Isaiah, who would redeem humanity by his own undeserved suffering. At a time when Israel was seething with revolt against Rome, Jesus took care not to identify himself with the revolutionary Zealots, and foresaw that the end of armed rebellion would be destruction rather than liberation: that when it came in 66 CE, the rebellion would 'not leave you one stone standing on another'. Jerusalem was destroyed, and after another rebellion later Israel ceased to exist.

Jesus' love was an active benevolence cutting across barriers of class, race and nation. In the Sermon on the Mount he taught his followers to love their enemies, to forgive those who had wronged them, and to respond to violence with non-violence, returning good for evil.

THE JUST WAR

T HE early Church took the teachings of Jesus literally, and opposed violence and killing for any purpose, but as the Church gradually became more involved in the affairs of state, its teachings began to change. When, in 324 CE, the Emperor Constantine made Christianity the state religion of the Roman Empire, the Church turned from pacifism and accepted the use of armed force by the state as justifiable. In time the Doctrine of the Just War was developed, and most of the Church has accepted this view, but the early pacifism of the Church later resurfaced in heretical movements like the Cathars and the Anabaptists.

For a war to be just, three conditions were laid down by St Thomas Aquinas in the thirteenth century:

a The war must only be started and controlled by the authority of the state or the ruler.

b There must be a just cause; those attacked are attacked because they deserve it.

c The war must be fought to promote good or avoid evil. Peace and justice must be restored afterwards.

Later two other conditions were added:

d The war must be the last resort; all other possible ways of solving the problem must have been tried out.

e There must be 'proportionality' in the way war is fought; for example, innocent civilians should not be killed. Only enough force may be used to achieve goals, not more. (It would not be 'proportionate', for example, to bomb a whole village because the enemy was hiding in one house.)

But can killing other beings ever be called 'just'?

If we apply the 'Just War' theory to the question of *whether it is morally justifiable to use nuclear weapons* we find that while some conditions may be met (although nuclear weapons could still be in the hands of non-governmental groups) other conditions are certainly not. Christian members of organizations such as CND argue that the Just War theory may have applied in the pre-nuclear world but in the nuclear, biological and chemical age modern weapons of mass destruction make a nonsense of the theory. There would be no justice afterwards – children (*if* there were any survivors) would be born with genetic defects for generations to come, and innocent civilians would be killed. Nuclear weapons do not prevent wars, and even though there are 36,000 nuclear weapons worldwide there is military conflict worldwide too.

If the decision is made that a Christian

may participate in war as a last resort, then the first decision must not involve an automatic legitimation of all and any methods. All methods of preventing war must first be tried and continued. Participation does not rule out the deepest personal abhorrence of violence. It might be thought, however, that the reality in the nuclear world rules out war completely. As more states acquire nuclear weapons, the danger of world annihilation increases. Even in a supposedly justifiable war there would be no justice left to preserve.

Against this thesis may be set the numerous arguments suggesting the tactical use of nuclear weapons in limited stages of war. In the face of complete lack of experience of such wars, it is impossible to predict consequences with certainty. Even here there are important grades of activity. It is clearly better to destroy military bases than centres of civilian population. It is clearly better to build nuclear shelters, if we may assume that they may give some degree of protection, than to pursue a policy which deliberately solves the problem of emergency food supply by ensuring that 50 per cent of the population will not survive an initial attack. Whatever we may think necessary in an extreme situation, there can be no doubt that any policy which results in the destruction of people is abhorrent (Fig. 10.2).

Fig. 10.2 Anti-nuclear protestors in India

THE ARMS TRADE ■

IT would cost $6 billion a year on top of what is already spent, to put every child in the world in school by 2003. That is an enormous sum. Yet it is less than one per cent of what the world spends on the military. In its recommendations to the British government in 1994 the Church of England urged an ethically responsible, transparent, publicly accountable and consistent arms trade policy, calling for:

The subordination of commercial criteria to political and ethical judgement; the clear separation between arms transfers and provision of aid: the refusal of arms transfers to countries engaged in, or likely to engage in, aggression: the refusal of arms transfers to regions of tension – except to countries adjudged by the international community to be under threat and insufficiently armed to be able effectively to exercise the right of self-defence (Article 51, UN Charter): the removal of direct and indirect government subsidies for arms transfers: the rejection of arms transfers to countries guilty of grave and consistent patterns of human rights violations, or involved in unnecessarily high levels of arms spending: the rejection of arms transfers to countries in breach of international law and those which refuse to participate in international arms control negotiations and respect international agreements: and support for an international ban on the production and transfer of anti-personnel mines, including prohibition of their export from the United Kingdom.

Some philosophers argue that to say war is sometimes necessary denies choice because ethics demands free choice and yet necessity denies choice. There may be reasons for waging war but they can never be *just* reasons as justice is defined by applying fairness and ensuring equality on both sides, which war cannot do.

A Just War sets such high moral standards that no state can follow them; *any* breach of the conditions lays the state open to the sort of challenge it purports to be fighting against. In modern warfare it is civilians who tend to suffer most, and despite military claims of 'clinical' strikes, civilians undoubtedly get killed, which straightaway violates the principles of proportionality and discrimination.

MILITARISM ■

THE glorification of war and heroic self-sacrifice in battle are the hallmarks of **militarism**, which is defined as 'the undue prevalence of the military spirit in society'. What are the *values* of militarism?

Fig. 10.3 The martial arts are taught to strengthen the body and train the spirit

he taught his disciples the idea of practising the martial arts, not for fighting but for strengthening the body and training the spirit. Before Bodhidharma came to China martial artists trained in order to fight, and were fond of bullying the weak; Bodhidharma introduced the concept of *wu-te* ('war-virtue', or 'martial spirit'), which taught that the martial arts are intended to promote spiritual development, not fighting.

Despite much misunderstanding, to this day millions of martial artists around the world find satisfaction and enrichment from the practice of a discipline which helps them to train and overcome their own aggressive impulses and find alternative strategies to violence in their daily lives.

HINDUISM AND NON-VIOLENCE

AHIMSA, non-injury, is a concept common to Buddhism, Hinduism and Jainism. First brought to prominence by the Jains, ahimsa was interpreted by them in an extreme form, with followers of the Jain religion going so far as to wear face-masks to prevent the accidental swallowing of insects, and sweeping their path before them to avoid stepping on any tiny creatures; some would even lie on bug-ridden mattresses to feed the bed-bugs.

In Hinduism non-injury was interpreted in a more pragmatic way – Hindus believe that this world is not conveniently arranged for the practice of absolute non-violence; we have to eliminate rats and cockroaches from our houses, as they carry disease; in times of war we must use force to defend our families from death and slavery. Though the use of force is evil, when employed against a greater evil such as a murderous tyrant, the lesser of the two evils becomes, in this relative world, an act of righteousness. But this is not a justification for the use of force or retaliation in any circumstances: there is a great difference between a righteous and an unrighteous war.

Hindus condone the use of force in a just defensive war against an invader, but still believe that spiritual power is superior to brute force. In the end wars lead to further wars, defeat to revenge, and the only way to defeat evil is through love. Good and evil are regarded as relative opposites in this world of duality; the power of love is beyond all opposites.

In the *Bhagavad Gita*, one of the most popular of Hindu Scriptures, the action takes place on a battlefield. The great warrior Arjuna experiences doubts about the righteousness of the battle he is about to fight, and his friend Krishna, the incarnation of God, teaches him the inner meaning of the battle of life. Although the story of the Gita is based on an historical battle which is thought to have taken place near Delhi in about 930 BCE, all the figures in the story represent qualities of the mind: thus Arjuna and his brothers represent spiritual qualities such as self-control, vitality and calm in battle, and their opponents represent Mr Ego, King Blind Mind, Prince Material Desire and all their followers. Krishna teaches Arjuna that he must fight the outer war against injustice in the same spirit that the yogi fights the inner war against the evil in his own mind. He must fight without hate or feelings of revenge, without attachment and without desire for the fruits of victory. Non-violence is of the mind, and it is the attitude of non-violence that is crucial, even in the midst of battle.

Gandhi and non-violence

Mahatma Gandhi (1869–1948) (Fig. 10.4) led the struggle for Indian independence, promoting ahimsa, non-injury, as a means of non-violent struggle, defining it as 'the avoidance of harm to any living creature in thought or deed'. Time after time Gandhi's followers resisted by non-cooperation laws that they considered unjust; they were mercilessly attacked and beaten, but repeatedly got to their feet and offered their broken skulls and limbs for further abuse. Their show of courage caused many of their attackers to throw down their weapons and refuse to beat those who, for the sake of their convictions, were not afraid of maiming or death.

Gandhi used non-violence as a political tactic to shame the British administration into granting freedom to India, but this tactic presupposes that the oppressor is capable of being touched by the promptings of conscience. Experience has shown – in South Africa, in the Soviet Union, in Tibet – that conscienceless oppressive dictatorships are incapable of being touched by an appeal to the heart.

It is sometimes thought that Gandhi taught a doctrine of absolute pacifism, the view that violence is never justified in any circumstances, but in fact he maintained that it is better to resist with physical force than to be a coward. If, for example, my family is threatened by armed robbers and I say to them, out of fear for my own life, 'I

Fig. 10.4 Mahatma Gandhi

forgive you for what you are about to do', and then walk away leaving my family to rape and butchery, then this is a display not of non-violence but of cowardice. Gandhi taught that a person in such a situation should resort to the use of necessary force rather than justify his or her cowardice through the philosophy of non-violence.

Literally speaking, ahimsa means 'non-killing'. But to me it has a world of meaning, and it takes me into realms much higher, infinitely higher. It really means that you may not harbour an uncharitable thought, even in connection with one who may consider himself to be your enemy.

Mahatma Gandhi

ISLAM AND THE HOLY WAR

ONE of the responsibilities of a practising Muslim is **jihad**, 'striving' (to serve Allah), usually translated in the west as 'Holy War', which Muslims agree is a fair translation. All Muslims must constantly wage jihad to the best of their ability, especially coming to the aid of any fellow Muslim attacked for practising Islam. Jihad, the defence of Islam, is regarded as just as much a primary duty of all sincere Muslims as prayer and fasting.

In the early years of the Islamic era jihad was interpreted as the armed struggle against pagans and non-believers, and the followers of Muhammad, fired by the teachings of the Prophet, swept out of Arabia to create an empire which eventually stretched from Spain to Indonesia. The fear created in Europe by the early successes of the armies of Islam still remains to this day, and many think that Islam is a religion of war and oppression, and hold the Muslims responsible for the brutalities of the much later Crusades.

In fact, the Crusaders were more like bands of thugs from the west who descended on the flourishing and peaceful civilizations of the Middle East, raping and butchering as they went. The first thing the supposed followers of Christ did when they got to the Middle East was to sack Constantinople, the capital of the Orthodox Church, and butcher their fellow Christians! In our own day western propaganda against Islam – Islamophobia – is partly an attempt to divert attention away from the crimes of the western powers in their treatment of Muslims.

The teaching of jihad in Islam is based on the teachings of the Qur'an, which, for the Muslim, is God's Revelation. The study and interpretation of the Qur'an proceeds from the outer literal meaning to the inner, spiritual meaning of the Revelation. The Qur'an teaches that the reason for our appearance in this world is to gain total knowledge of things; to become perfected as the 'Universal Man'; the purpose of the creation is for God to come to know Himself through the perfect instrument of knowledge which is the 'Universal Man'. God wished to know Himself, to see His qualities – power, mercy, intelligence, beauty – reflected in the Creation, so He created human beings as the instrument of His self-knowledge. Thus, through struggle (jihad) we become a mirror reflecting the Divine Names and Qualities, enabling God to fulfil the purpose of His Creation. The inner meaning of the Holy War is the struggle with our own evil and the victory over our own inner darkness.

HOW TO STOP WARS ▬▬

IS it possible to end wars? The spiritual teacher and writer George Gurdjieff (1866–1949) in *In Search of the Miraculous* taught that without self-knowledge humankind remained a slave of forces beyond its control:

Wars cannot be stopped. War is the result of the slavery in which men live. Strictly speaking men are not to blame for war. War is due to cosmic forces, to planetary influences. But in men there is no resistance whatever against these influences, and there cannot be any, because men are slaves. If they were men they would be capable of 'doing', they would be able to resist these influences and refrain from killing one another.

For Gurdjieff some of the causes of war are inside ourselves, some are outside ourselves. We must begin with the causes that are in us. Freedom, liberation, is our aim, and to become free we must be liberated from slavery. At the moment our beliefs and our behaviour are controlled by everything around us: by advertising, by political propaganda, even by the weather. But we cannot be free outwardly while we remain slaves inwardly, and the only path to inner freedom is through self-knowledge. Without self-knowledge we cannot be free and will remain the plaything of the forces acting on us. This is why the demand at the beginning of the road to freedom is: 'Know thyself'.

EXAM QUESTIONS

1 On what basis could one assert that it is morally obligatory to use violence in order to defend the weak?   [EDEXCEL, 1998]

2 Is absolute pacifism defensible? Give reasons for your answer.
      [Oxford and Cambridge, 1998]

3 'You are just as dead if killed by a bullet as you are from being vaporised by a five megaton nuclear blast.' Does this fact prove that the moral issues concerning nuclear warfare are no different from those concerning conventional warfare?
      [EDEXCEL, 1997]

4 'Pacifism is an irresponsible pipe dream. There will always be occasions when wars have to be fought.' Discuss.
      [EDEXCEL, 1996]

5 Is the term *Just War* now out-dated? Give reasons for your answer.
      [Oxford and Cambridge, 1997]

Further reading

Aldridge S. 'Ethical Dilemmas', in *New Scientist*, 114, October 1998

British Humanist Association, *Thinking About Ethical Issues*, 1996

Bremner, Moyra, 'Mammon Gone Mad', *Caduceus*, Summer 1998

Brown, D., *Choices: Ethics and The Christian*, Blackwell, 1983

Cook, D., *The Moral Maze*, SPCK, 1993

Dilemmas in Medicine, RE 16+ A Cross-Curricular Course, Christian Education Movement Wales (CEMW), Mudiad Addysg Gristnogol Cymru, 1997

Divisive Barbarity or Global Civilization? The Ethical Dimensions of Science, Art, Religion and Politics, University Press of Maryland, 1996

Examining Religious Moral Issues in Six Religions, ed., Owen Cole, Heinemann, 1992

Fletcher, J., *Situation Ethics*, SCM Press, 1966

Fox, M., *The Coming of the Cosmic Christ*, New York, HarperCollins, 1988

Frankena, W.K., *Ethics*, Prentice Hall, 1973

Jenkins, J., *Christianity*, Heinemann, 1995
Contemporary Moral Issues, Heinemann, 1997

King, Martin Luther, *Strength to Love*, Hodder & Stoughton, 1970

La Follette, H., (ed.), *Ethics in Practice: An Anthology*, Blackwell, 1997

Life in Christ: Morals, Communions and the Church, An Agreed Statement by the Second Anglican-Roman Catholic International Commission, Church House Publishing and Catholic Truth Society, 1994

Mackie, J. L., *Ethics: Inventing Right and Wrong*, Penguin, 1981

Macquarrie, J. and Childress, J. (eds), *A New Dictionary of Christian Ethics*, SCM Press, 1986

Monbiot, George (ed), 'The Gene Debate', *Resurgence*, May/June 1998

Nuttall, J. *Moral Questions: An Introduction to Ethics*, Blackwell, 1993

Ouspensky, P. D., *In Search of the Miraculous*, London, Routledge & Kegan Paul, 1950

Rachels, J., *The Elements of Moral Philosophy*, McGraw-Hill, 1995

Real Philosophy: An Anthology of The Universal Search for Meaning, with introduction and commentary by Jacob Needleman and David Applebaum, Arkana, 1990

Robinson, D. and Garratt, C., *Ethics for Beginners*, Icon Books, 1996

Russell, B., *History of Western Philosophy*, George Allen & Unwin, 1946

Shaw, A. and Bonner Steel, A., *Liberation, RE 16+ A Cross-Curricular Course*, Christian Education Movement Wales (CEMW), 1998

Singer, P., *Practical Ethics*, University of Cambridge, 1979
How Are We to Live: Ethics in an Age of Self-interest, Mandarin, 1995
(ed.) *A Companion to Ethics*, Blackwell, 1993

Smith, D., *Life and Morality: Contemporary Medico-moral Issues*, Gill and MacMillan, 1996

The New Internationalist, 'How are we to live?', April 1997

Thompson, M., *Teach Yourself Ethics*, Hodder & Stoughton, 1994

Universal Declaration of Human Rights, United Nations Association Wales

Vardy, P. and Grosch, P., *The Puzzle of Ethics*, Fount Paperbacks, 1994

Warnock, M., *An Intelligent Person's Guide to Ethics*, Duckworth, 1998

Wright, C. and Augarde, T. (eds), *Peace is the Way: A Guide to Pacifist Views and Actions*, Lutterworth Press, 1990

Yogananda, P., *God Talks With Arjuna: The Bhagavad Gita*, Self-Realization Fellowship, 1995

Glossary

Note – words appearing in **bold** within an entry have their own entry elsewhere in the glossary.

Absolute Perfect in quality; complete; not limited by restrictions or exceptions. This term is often applied to God but can also be applied to 'truth'.

Absolutism The theory that morality is **absolute** rather than relative (see **relativism**): i.e. that there are **moral** truths which we must adhere to and which particular situations, people, or places do not affect.

Act-utilitarianism Theory according to which the rightness or wrongness of individual acts are calculated by the amount of happiness resulting from these acts.

Agape Understanding, creative and redemptive goodwill to all people. An overflowing of love that seeks nothing in return. Theologians call it the love of God operating in the human heart.

Agapeistic Calculus 'There is only one duty and this is to "love thy neighbour as thyself".'

Agribusiness Commercial farming on an industrial scale, financed by corporations rather than individuals.

Ahimsa The Indian principle of avoiding harm to any living creature in thought or deed.

Altruism Considering other people's happiness before one's own.

Amoral Indifferent to morality. Babies are considered amoral, as are adults who are severely mentally disturbed or those who have had prefrontal lobotomies. Amoral can also mean not knowing the difference between right and wrong.

Anthropocentrism Belief that the non-human world only has value insofar as it is instrumental in satisfying human desires.

Autonomy The power of self-determination and freedom from alien domination and constraint. Autonomy in **ethics** focuses on the individual's capacity for self-determination.

Avarice Greedy eagerness and desire for wealth.

Benevolence An attitude of goodwill.

Bioethics The application of **ethics** to the biological sciences, medicine, health care and related areas.

Biotechnology The exploitation of biological processes for industrial and other purposes especially **genetic** manipulation of micro-organisms.

Categorical Imperative 'I ought to do such and such regardless of my own wishes.' The key principle of Kant's **ethics**, which states essentially that an act is **immoral** if the rule which would authorize it cannot be made into a rule for all human beings.

Censorship The scrutiny of material (literature, plays, films, etc.) before it is released into the public domain; acting as a filter to prevent what is undesirable ever reaching the public.

Christofascists Christian fundamentalist whose fundamentalist interpretation of Christian values blinds them to the realities of true Christian values such as equality, justice for all and religious tolerance.

Classical utilitarianism Right actions are those that produce the greatest balance of happiness over unhappiness.

Cloning Making a copy, replicating. Basically there are two applications of cloning techniques: (1) as a reproductive method and (2) as a regenerative method (i.e. life-saving tissue generation for medical purposes such as transplants).

Collective responsibility When all members of an identifiable group are answerable for events, persons or conditions connected with the group as an entity.

Compassion An emotional attitude towards another person, characteristically involving an active regard for the other person's good.

Conscientious objection A form of dissent against an institution's rules, policies or practices; often refers to refusal to participate in military service on ethical or religious grounds.

Consequentialism Ethical theories which are concerned with the consequences of actions or rules. The traditional philosophical name for this is teleology (see **teleological theories**); from the Greek *telos* meaning end or purpose.

Cultural absolutism The belief that there is a **universal moral** order at work and that some ethical beliefs are identical irrespective of differing cultural beliefs and practices.

Cultural relativism The belief that ethical values depend upon, and vary with, cultural conditioning and **moral** training, and so no moral belief system can be **universally** true.

Decalogue The Ten Commandments a collection of ten short, primarily negative, guidelines for human conduct, presented in the Hebrew Bible as God's revelation to Moses on Mount Sinai.

Deep Ecology The belief that all nature, including humanity's, is a unified whole, and that any change to a natural system by human activity is unlikely to be harmful to that system. Opposes **anthropocentrism**.

Dehumanization The process whereby human beings, either individually or socially, are oppressed and unable to develop their potential as human beings or societies of human beings.

Deontological theories **Ethical** theories that maintain that an action is good or bad,

right or wrong, by something within the action itself. (*Deon* comes from the Greek meaning 'duty'.)

Determinism The belief that acts of will, natural events, or social changes are settled and decided by earlier causes.

Dharma Indian principle of **universal moral** order.

Divine Command theory An act is morally right if God has commanded it and morally wrong if God has forbidden it.

DNA Complex two stranded molecule that contains, in chemically coded form, all the information needed to build, control and maintain a living organism.

Duty ethics The name sometimes attributed to Kant's system of **ethics** because of his stress on performing a **moral** act out of a sense of duty rather than inclination.

Egoism Theory concerned with self-interest. The word 'egoism' is often used in a **pejorative** sense to mean 'excessive self-regard'.

Egoistic Hedonism To act only in your own interest to get maximum satisfaction.

Emotivism The **moral** theory based on people's emotive response to other people, situations, principles and viewpoints.

Empathy Imagining oneself to be another person so as to share their feelings and ideas ('standing in someone else's shoes').

Environmental ethics Concerned with issues arising out of human interaction with the environment.

Equality Although we are all different in terms of physique, skills, etc in some ultimate ontological sense we are all equal and this equality is more important than any empirical differences.

Ethicist A person who 'does' **ethics** in the sense of reflecting on morality, its nature, its presuppositions and its application.

Ethics From the Greek *ethos* meaning 'character'. In this book ethics is used interchangeably with morality. In philosophy ethics means the study of morality. There are two approaches to ethics: the scientific (or descriptive), as used by social science, and the philosophical, which includes **normative ethics** and **meta-ethics**. When used in its ordinary sense, however, ethics, like morality, means the values by which human beings live in relation to other human beings, nature, God, and/or themselves.

Ethnocentrism Evaluating other races and cultures by criteria specific to one's own race and or culture.

Eugenics The science or practice of altering a human population by controlled breeding for 'desirable' inherited characteristics.

Euthanasia The painless termination of human life for the purpose of ending severe physical suffering.

Euthyphro's dilemma 'Is conduct right because the gods command it or do the gods command it because it is right?'

Existentialist ethics Making a virtue out of not knowing what to do. Living by laws (which is a way of knowing what to do) is regarded by existentialists as 'bad faith'.

Feminist ethics Refers to any ethical theory that located its roots in feminism – the conviction and movement opposed to discrimination on the basis of gender.

Formula of the End in Itself One of Kant's formulations of the **Categorical Imperative**: Act in such a way that you always treat humanity, whether in your own person or in the person of any other, never simply as a means, but always at the same time an end. It is never right to treat people just as a means to some end – human beings are always 'ends in themselves'.

Formula of Universal Law One of Kant's formulations of the **Categorical Imperative**: Act as if the maxim of your action was to become through your will a universal law of nature, i.e. we should act in such a way that we can will that the **maxim** under which we act should be a general law for everyone.

Free will Human actions are the result of free rational choice on the part of agents, who are not compelled to act by forces outside of their **moral** consciousness.

Freudianism Theory which states that human beings are determined by inner drives and unconscious motivations to behave the way they do.

Gaia Hypothesis Theory that the earth's living and non-living systems form an inseparable whole that is regulated and kept adapted for life by living organisms themselves. The planet functions therefore as a single organism.

Gene splicing Technique for inserting a foreign gene into laboratory cultures of bacteria to generate commercial biological products such as synthetic insulin, hepatitis B vaccine and interferon.

Genetically modified (GM) foods Food products that have been genetically engineered or that contain genetically engineered ingredients.

Geneticism Prejudice against persons or potential persons who do not meet certain genetic requirements. The inhumane striving for a 'genetic elite'.

Genetics The study of human variability in terms of its causes and effects.

Genocide The deliberate and systematic destruction of a racial, political or cultural group.

Genotype The particular variants of genes possessed by a given organism.

Germline gene therapy In theory, a disease can be treated by removing the faulty gene responsible for the disease and replacing it with a normal one, whereby the corrected genes may be passed on to future generations.

Golden Rule The principle common to all world faiths that we should treat others as we would wish to be treated.

Good An action is judged 'right' or 'wrong' depending upon whether or not it is a 'good' or 'bad' thing to do. 'Good' can be defined in **absolute** terms (it is good in its particular context). It can also be defined in what it can achieve, so an action is 'good' if the result of that action are 'good'. Aristotle describes good as something which fulfils its purpose. (This formed the basis of the **Natural Law** approach to ethics.)

Grace   the state of the soul when freed from evil; the mercy and help of God.

Hedonism   A term used to describe an attitude which makes happiness the goal of life. *Hedone* is the Greek word for pleasure.

Humanistic ethics   'Humans are the measure of things'. Humans, not God, have the sole responsibility for bettering and fulfilling their existence in this world.

Hypothetical imperatives   'If you want to play professional football, practice your skills.' Hypothetical imperatives are based on an 'if'. We can reject the command to practise if we resist the 'if' on which the command rests. **Moral** imperatives, by contrast, do not depend upon our having particular desires – they are **categorical**.

Immoral   That which is bad or wrong such as a bad person or a wrong action; used interchangeably in this book with 'unethical'.

Institutionalized racism   The collective failure of an organization to provide an appropriate and professional service to people because of their colour, culture, or ethnic origin. It can be seen or detected in processes, attitudes and behaviour which amount to discrimination through unwitting **prejudice**, ignorance, thoughtlessness and racist stereotyping which disadvantages minority ethnic people.

Intuitionism   Basic **moral** principles are understood by intuition – they are self-evident and one only has to consider them in order to recognize the truth.

Islamic ethics   Based on religious sources, primarily the Qur'an, the scripture of Islam, supported and expanded by the Hadith (traditions of Muhammad). Emphasis is on conformity to the Law: an action is commanded or forbidden by God – all aspects of life are regulated by the Shari'a – the religious law.

Islamophobia   A climate of distrust of and **prejudice** against the Muslim community.

Jihad   'Holy war' (Islamic). A jihad may be undertaken to defend Islam against external threats or spread the religion among non-believers. The term is also used to mean effort in the cause of God and can encompass struggle against resistance to the rule of divine law within oneself.

Justice   As rational beings we should treat others as we would like to be treated unless there is some reasonable ground for difference in treatment.

Kingdom of Ends   One of Kant's formulations of the **Categorical Imperative** on which all **moral** commands are based: 'So act as if you were through your **maxims** a law – making member of a Kingdom of Ends'. Kant envisages rational agents acting as if they were making laws for themselves based on reason. By doing this they will become 'law-making members of a Kingdom of Ends'. The laws adopted by all members will be the same because they are all based on reason. If there are disagreements rational discussions should be able to resolve these.

Kingdom of God   Expresses a conception of God's being, benevolence, omniscience, omnipresence and omnipotence. This theological concept has been reinterpreted by some Christians as an ethical term signifying social justice and freedom for the oppressed.

Legalism   A type of **ethic** that seeks to prescribe rules for every conceivable occasion of **moral** choice.

Living Will   A will by which healthy and mentally competent people can inform their relatives and others of how they want to be treated or not treated when they are too sick or incompetent to decide such things.

Logical Positivism   The only meaningful propositions are those that can be verified empirically; and those that cannot are neither true nor false, but simply meaningless.

Maxim   A general principle.

Meta-ethics   The analysis of ethical language.

Militarism   The undue prevalence of the military spirit in society; the glorification of war and heroic self-sacrifice in battle are the hallmarks of militarism.

Moral That which is good or right, such as a good person or a right action. Used interchangeably in this book with ethical.

Natural Law theory Theory that everything is created for a particular purpose and fulfilling this purpose is the 'good' to which everything aims.

Naturalistic ethics Theories which seek to reduce all ethical concepts to concepts of natural science.

Naturalistic theories of ethics Theories which hold that goodness can be defined in terms of some **non-moral** position, e.g. pleasure, or the good of society.

Non-moral That which is completely out of the sphere of morality. Animals, plants and inanimate objects are essentially non-moral.

Normative ethics The setting up of norms or value-systems which prescribe how human beings ought or should behave (also known as prescriptive ethics). All ethical systems such as ethical **egoism**, **Natural Law theory**, **Utilitarianism** and Kant's **Duty ethics** are normative.

Objective Outside or external to us rather than within us (see **subjective**).

Objective morality Principles that are the same for all people everywhere and at all times.

Obligations Responsibilities we have towards one another (by morality, laws or traditions) to see that the just **rights** of others are protected.

Pacifist Someone who believes that it is wrong to harm or kill other people, and that if killing is wrong, then war must be wrong, as war is basically a matter of killing.

Pejorative Implies that somebody or someone is worthless.

Personhood That point at which a human being can be considered as having a personality and able to enter into relationships with others and with the external world.

Philia Intimate love between friends.

Prejudice An injury, detriment or damage caused to a person by judgements or actions that disregard his or her **rights**; 'a previous judgement' due to a preconceived opinion.

Prenatal diagnosis the ability of medical technology to diagnose diseases and genetic disorders before birth (e.g. ultrasound imaging or amniocentesis).

Prescriptivist A name commonly given to those with views which hold that **moral** judgements are in some special sense 'action-guiding'.

Prima facie duty A duty 'at first glance'; i.e. all other things being equal, we ought to do it.

Professional ethics A profession is not just about making a living, but involves honesty, trust, responsibility to others, standards and integrity. The earliest known instance of a 'professional code' is the Hippocratic Oath (c. 4 BCE).

Psychological egoism 'Everyone will ultimately do what is in their own self-interest.'

Reductionism The tendency to, or principle of, analysing complex things down into simple parts.

Relativism The theory that morality is relative rather than **absolute**: i.e. that morality can differ in different cultures at different times.

Responsibility From the Latin *respondere*, 'to answer' – inferring accountability, being answerable for one's actions.

Rights Powers or privileges to which an individual has a just claim such that she or he can demand that they not be infringed or suspended. Rights involve a mutual recognition on the part of each individual of the claims or rights of others. Rights are thus correlated with duties.

Rule-utilitarianism If following a rule will result in more happiness than not following a rule then we should adopt the rule as a **moral** principle and always act in accordance with it.

Secularism The belief that human beings are capable of handling their affairs without evoking a god. The disengagement of institutions, practices and activities from religion.

Seven deadly sins The sins of pride,

covetousness (**avarice**, or greed), lust, gluttony, envy, anger and sloth.

Situation Ethics Theory that the only ethical principle applicable to all situations is love.

Social contract The view that 'society' originated when individuals agreed to surrender some of their 'natural **rights**' and social **obligation** was born.

Socialism An ideal, a vision of a day when **equality**, **justice**, fraternity and liberty will all find full expression in society.

Speceism A **prejudice** towards the interests of one's own species as against the interests of other species.

Stewardship The concept that we are trustees of creation and cannot escape the **obligation** to act responsibly.

Subjective Coming from within us rather than from outside (see **objective**).

Subjective morality 'What one person calls good another calls bad': the belief that morality is different in different countries or cultures and at different times.

Summum bonum A final value which is desirable in itself and not merely desirable as a means to an end.

Tautological statement An unnecessary repetition of the same idea in different words (e.g. 'he sat alone by himself') which does not make the meaning clearer.

Teleological theories Theories in which actions are judged good or bad by reference to the end to which they aim.

Transgenics A form of genetic engineering which introduces new **DNA** to breed functionally specific plants, animals or bacteria. Those organisms with a foreign gene added are said to be transgenic.

Unity in Diversity A view which attempts to resolve the **absolutism/relativism** controversy we are all similar yet different; and should strive for unity.

Universal Applicable to all human beings, situations and places. A **moral rule** which is 'universalizable' is one which is capable of being applied to all human beings without self-contradiction.

Utilitarianism Belief that an action is right if it has consequences that lead to happiness, and wrong if it brings about the reverse. Thus society should aim for the greatest happiness of the greatest number.

Virtue Any kind of excellence (translated from the Greek *arete*).

Vows A definite promise; an undertaking whereby a person binds himself or herself to do or not to do; or to give something by a promise.

Index